Making Sense

Making Sense:

The Glamorous Story of English Grammar

David Crystal

OXFORD

UNIVERSITY PRESS

OXFORD
UNIVERSITY PRESS

Oxford University Press is a department of the University of Oxford.
It furthers the University's objective of excellence in research, scholarship,
and education by publishing worldwide. Oxford is a registered trade mark of
Oxford University Press in the UK and certain other countries.

Published in the United States of America by Oxford University Press
198 Madison Avenue, New York, NY 10016, United States of America.

Library of Congress Cataloging-in-Publication Data
Names: Crystal, David, 1941- author.
Title: Making sense : the glamorous story of English grammar / David
Crystal.
Description: First edition. | Oxford University Press : Oxford ; New York,
[2017] | Includes bibliographical references and index.
Identifiers: LCCN 2016050472 (print) | LCCN 2017005444 (ebook) |
ISBN 9780190660574 (cloth : alk. paper) | ISBN 9780190660581 (pdf) |
ISBN 9780190660598 (ebook)
Subjects: LCSH: English language—Grammar—Theory, etc. | English
language—Grammar—Study and teaching (Higher) | Linguistic change. |
English language—Variation. | English language—Spoken English.
Classification: LCC PE1095 .C79 2017 (print) | LCC PE1095 (ebook) |
DDC 425—dc23
LC record available at https://lccn.loc.gov/2016050472

1 3 5 7 9 10 8 6 4 2
Printed by Edwards Brothers, United States of America

Contents

Preface

As with the earlier titles in this series, on spelling (*Spell It Out*) and punctuation (*Making a Point*), my aim in this book is exactly what its title and subtitle suggest: to explain how the subject of grammar has evolved since classical times to reach the position it is in today. All three books – to coin a phrase, S, P a[nd] G – bring to light the complex history of the English language, which is calling out for description at a point when our present-day sensibilities are struggling to grasp the realities of language variation and change, and the implications this has for children's education.

Grammar presents a special challenge, because – far more than in the case of spelling and punctuation – there is so much abstract terminology to take on board, and the subject is burdened with a centuries-old history of educational practice that many readers will recall as being anything but glamorous. The obvious questions therefore are: Where did it all come from? Why is it needed? What is its value? How can it be taught – and tested? And where on earth could glamour possibly lie?

I address all these questions in this book, while bearing in mind that my readership will range from those who already have considerable expertise to those with little or no grammatical knowledge. The opening chapters have two parts, accordingly: an opening section that is introductory in character; and an explanatory section that explores each issue in greater depth. Taken together, I hope these will provide a satisfying answer to the question I am most often asked: 'Why is there such a fuss about grammar?'

I am most grateful to those who read a draft of the book from various points of view: to Professor Richard Hudson, especially for providing me with extra perspective on recent UK trends in language in education; to Hilary Crystal, for advice on my general level and approach to the subject; and to John Davey (who commissioned the work on behalf of Profile Books) for guidance on matters of content and organization.

Chapters on the political background to grammar-teaching in the UK were felt by the publisher to be too parochial for an international readership, so I have made these available on my website as an essay entitled 'The recent political history of English grammar in the UK': www.davidcrystal.com

grammar

from Old French *gramaire,*
which was an adaptation of Latin *grammatica*
which in turn came from Greek *grammatiki*
meaning 'pertaining to letters or literature'
which later narrowed to mean just the language of texts
which in the Middle Ages meant chiefly Latin
and so took on the meaning of 'special learning, knowledge'
and then 'secret knowledge' as in magic and astrology
which is how it was first used in Scotland in the 18th century
when the word was pronounced with an *l* instead of an *r*
and the meaning developed of 'enchantment, spell'
and later became the word we know today, meaning
'charm, attractiveness, physical allure'
spelled

glamour (British English)
glamor (American English)

Introduction

Not knowing grammar: a student's tale

I was giving a new intake of undergraduates their first lecture on English grammar. It was the early 1970s – a few years after the formal teaching of grammar had disappeared from the school curriculum in the UK, and I was about to experience one of the consequences.

I'd given this course several times. The main aim of my opening lecture was to make students aware of the contrast between the 'old' ways of learning about grammar they had experienced in school and the new approaches they would encounter at university. To do this, I would take an example of a rule I knew they would all have been taught: 'Never end a sentence with a preposition.' Many older readers will recall having had that rule dinned into them.

I'll explain where the rule came from in Chapter 12. In my class I simply illustrated what the rule did. They would have been told that the first of the following two sentences was 'incorrect', and the second was 'correct':

This is the man I was talking to.
This is the man to whom I was talking.

I would then go on to show how sentences with prepositions at the end have been used in English since Anglo-Saxon times, give some examples from Shakespeare ('To

be or not to be ... and fly to others that I know not of'),
and point out that today the difference is one of style: the
second sentence is much more formal than the first. Both
are acceptable in standard English, but the first is more
likely to be found in informal speech and the second in
formal writing. Today I'd add that you don't see the second
one much on Facebook.

Anyway, on that day in the early 1970s, I was halfway
through my usual explanation when I noticed that my audience had begun to fidget (more than usual). Some were whis-
pering to each other. I stopped what I was saying and asked:
'Is there a problem?'

One student put her hand up. 'Please,' she said, 'What's
a preposition?'

I was, as I used to say in Liverpool, gobsmacked. I had
never been asked that question before. It had never occurred
to me that someone, now aged 18, could have gone through
school without learning what a preposition was. I asked the
audience: 'How many of you don't know what a preposition
is?' Most put their hands up. I couldn't believe it.

'I think I know,' said another student. 'Thank goodness,'
I thought, and asked her to continue. Then she said: 'Is it
something to do with getting on a horse?'

There is no single word in Liverpudlian slang for a greater
degree of gobsmackedness. I think I croaked, 'How do you
mean?'

'Well,' she said, 'I was always told that a pre-position was
what one had to adopt when preparing to mount.' She pronounced it 'pree-position'.

It was the first time I realized how great the change had
been in schools. Within just a few years – less than a decade
– many students were leaving school with no knowledge of
grammar at all. It seems that the teaching of grammar just

– stopped. I discovered later that it wasn't just a British thing. A similar disaffection had taken place in other mother-tongue countries where 'English' was a classroom subject. A few schools kept it going, especially in relation to the teaching of Latin or a modern language – which is why some of my class smugly knew what a preposition was – but in relation to English, it was as if grammar had never been.

I'll talk later about why all this happened and what replaced it. But the consequences of this radical change of direction were long-lasting. When grammar began to re-emerge in schools in the 1990s – in Britain, as part of the National Curriculum – there was a widespread uncertainty among teachers about how to handle it, for the obvious reason that these teachers had never had any grammatical training themselves. That uncertainty continues today.

It isn't just teachers. Parents too – those who have never had any grammar training either – are nonplussed when their child now turns to them for homework help and asks 'What's a preposition?' – or an adverb, or a noun phrase, or a subordinate clause ... And indeed, anyone who tries to speak or write clear and effective English can be nonplussed when they try to take on board the misleading advice offered by pedants who reduce grammar to a simple set of rights and wrongs and then insist on everyone else doing the same. Pedants need to make sense of grammar too.

We all do. Even little children.

Not knowing grammar: a child's tale

Suzie, aged eighteen months, came rushing excitedly into the room, clutching her favourite teddy bear, and stood there in front of me. 'Push!' she said, with a big smile on her face. I reflected, then bent down and gave her a gentle shove. She wobbled back a few paces, then looked at me with a big frown. 'No. Push!' she insisted.

I reflected again. I must have got it wrong. She wanted to push *me*. So I crouched down in front of her, opened my arms wide, and said, 'OK. Push me! Push me!' She stood there, even more serious and puzzled. 'No. Push!'

Eventually we worked it out. She took me by the hand, and we went into the next room, where there was a toy swing. She put teddy on the swing, turned to me, and said again, 'Push.' So that was it. It was teddy who needed the action.

I remember stupidly saying to her, at that point, 'So why didn't you say that in the first place?' And if she could have spoken, she would have said to me: 'Because, you prat, I'm only eighteen months old, and I haven't got any grammar yet.'

She might have continued: 'Ask me again in six months time, Daddy, and I'll show you some real grammar.' And that's what happened. At around age two, she was able to say such things as 'You push me', 'Me push you', and 'You push teddy in there.' In just a short time she had mastered the basic rules of word order in English sentences.

And what were these rules doing? They were helping her to make sense – to avoid the ambiguity of her earlier utterances. By 'make' here I mean, literally, 'construct', 'create'. Words by themselves do not make sense. They express a meaning, of course, but it's a vague sort of meaning. Only by putting words into real sentences do we begin to make sense. We begin to understand each other clearly and precisely, thanks to grammar, because grammar is the study of how sentences work.

That's the chief reason grammar exists: to make sense of words. And this book is about how we do that, the challenges people have faced trying to do that, why the task of speaking and writing in a grammatical way can get us into trouble, and how we can get ourselves out of that trouble. In short: I want to make sense of how we make sense.

E. Nesbit's *The Phoenix and the Carpet* (1904) opens with the children talking about the quality of their fireworks:

'The ones I got are all right,' Jane said; 'I know they are, because the man at the shop said they were worth thribble the money –'

'I'm sure thribble isn't grammar,' Anthea said.

'Of course it isn't,' said Cyril; 'one word can't be grammar all by itself, so you needn't be so jolly clever.'

1
First steps in grammar

All of Suzie's early words were ambiguous in one way or another. If she said *gone*, I had to note the situation where she used the word in order to work out what she was talking about. It might be something dropped on the floor, or someone leaving the room, or the TV being turned off. *Down* could mean that something had fallen down or she wanted to get down (from her high chair). *More* sometimes meant 'I do want some more' (food) as well as 'I don't want any more'. Even when she named things – and over half her early vocabulary consisted of names of people or objects – there was ambiguity. A dog was *dog*, but so were a cat and a bird, for a while.

And yet, despite this lack of grammatical sophistication, these utterances were nonetheless sentences, not just isolated words. Suzie was saying them with a definite rhythm and melody, and everyone responded to them as if they were real sentences.

Dada, said with a rising pitch, meant 'Is that Daddy?' Said with a falling pitch it meant 'There's Daddy'. Said with a level pitch (and arms outstretched) it meant 'Pick me up, Daddy'. The different pitch patterns made them sound like a question, a statement, and a command – even though there was no sign of the grammar we associate with these three types of sentence. This was a clear contrast with the rather random vocalizations Suzie had been making a few months before, when she was babbling away, and nobody could work out what she was saying. Old grammars used to say that 'a sentence expresses a complete thought'. Suzie certainly sounded as if she was expressing her first complete thoughts.

'First words', then, are really 'first sentences' – but sentences without any internal structure. Suzie also said something that sounded like 'awgaw', in a sing-song way. It was a childish pronunciation of what we often said to her at the end of a meal – *all gone*. To us, that sentence contained two separate words, but Suzie used it as if it were just one: *allgone*. This happened a lot. *Up and down* (a bouncing game) became *upandown*. For a while, she thought our dog's name was *gudaw* – 'good dog'.

Linguists have devised a technical term for these primitive one-word sentences. They call them *holophrases* (the first element is from a Greek word meaning 'whole'). They are a universal feature of language acquisition at this age. Regardless of the language children are learning, between twelve and eighteen months they will all go through a holophrastic stage. And, of course, if they're hearing more than one language routinely at home, they will do the same sort of thing with whatever words they pick up. At this age, children don't know that the words belong to different languages.

Keyword: sentence

What Suzie did between twelve and eighteen months is what we all have to do when we begin to explore English grammar – or the grammar of any language. Grammar is the study of the way we bring words together in order to make sense. These combinations of words make up larger constructions that we call phrases, clauses, sentences, paragraphs ... and grammar studies all of this: how they are constructed, and the meanings and effects that the various constructions convey.

Suzie needed grammar to make sense of her words. And so do we all. Isolated words don't usually make sense. If I suddenly come out with 'Thursday' or 'Indefatigable' or 'Sausages', my listeners will have no idea what I'm talking about. They will look around for some context that might help to explain what's in my mind, and if they don't find any they will conclude that there's something wrong with me – for indeed, speaking in isolated words can be a sign of mental disturbance.

Of all the constructions that we can make, the one that dominates the history of grammar is the sentence. Sentences make sense. That is their job. When we hear or see a sentence, the way it is constructed should convey a meaning that makes sense without having to ask for help. Sentences stand on their own two feet. They have a certain independence. This is the basis of the notion that a sentence needs to feel complete. It led to the old definition I mentioned above: 'a sentence expresses a complete thought'. That was never a good definition because who could ever say what a 'complete thought' was?

Take the sentence I wrote in the last paragraph:

It led to the old definition I mentioned above: 'a sentence expresses a complete thought'.

How many thoughts are there in that? The colon brings together two thoughts, in fact, one on each side. But as the word 'It' refers back to the previous sentence, maybe that should be included as well, making three. And as 'above' refers back to the beginning of this chapter, maybe that should be allowed in too, making four. Or maybe the thought is incomplete, as I need the other sentences in that paragraph to explain what I'm trying to say. Perhaps it's a paragraph that is a complete thought, then? Or a chapter? Or a book?

There *is* a feeling of completeness when we reach the end of a sentence, but it is a completeness that comes from the way the sentence is constructed, not from the thoughts that are in it. The sentences are said to be 'grammatically complete'. Most of the sentences on this page are. The following aren't:

> a very large tree
> walking down the road
> I saw a car and

To make them grammatical, we need to add some structure, such as:

> A very large tree was blocking the road.
> Walking down the road, we sang songs.
> I saw a car and a bus.

We show this completeness in writing by using a mark of final punctuation, such as a full stop. We show it in speech using patterns of definite intonation. Say one of those complete sentences aloud, and you will say it with a pitch pattern that tells your listener your sentence has come to an end. This was the very first feature of English that Suzie learned: how to make a sentence sound finished, so that a listener will respond to it.

It's actually quite difficult to give a definition of a sentence that handles all the ways in which sentences are constructed. If you've been brought up to believe that 'A sentence begins with a capital letter and ends with a full stop', then you have to think again when you encounter sentences that begin with a lower-case letter (as in millions of emails and social media posts, and quite a lot of poetry) and end with something other than a full stop, such as a question mark or exclamation mark ... or no punctuation mark at all, as in much public signage.

Or three dots, to express dramatic anticipation. It was a favourite stylistic trick of Agatha Christie, who frequently ends a chapter with 'ellipsis dots'. Here's the last paragraph of Chapter 17 of a Hercules Poirot novel, *Mrs McGinty's Dead*:

'Don't go in there – don't go in. Your mother – she – she's dead – I think – she's been killed ...'

And Chapter 18 takes up the cue in its opening line:

'Quite a neat bit of work,' said Superintendent Spence.

And note that the Superintendent's sentence actually ends with a comma – normal practice when writing direct speech.

We also have to allow for sentences that look or sound finished, yet their sense depends on other sentences around them. If you ask me 'Where is John going?' and I answer 'To the station' or 'He's going to town', I've replied using sentences, but they're of a rather special kind. My sentences follow the rules of English grammar, but they need your sentence in order to make complete sense. I used a couple earlier in this chapter: 'Or a chapter? Or a book?'

Grammarians use the term *elliptical* (from a Greek word meaning 'coming short') to describe sentences like 'To the station'. A pronoun such as *he* is said to be *anaphoric* (from a Greek word meaning 'carrying back'), as it refers back to the previous sentence. Why so many Greek-derived terms? See the following Interlude.

Despite these complications, the notion of a sentence has survived as a major concept in the study of grammar. We can approach it 'bottom up', starting with words and showing how words combine to make sentences. Or we can approach it 'top down', starting with some general definition of a sentence, and seeing how the words work within it. Either way, it's clear that there are a large number of ways in which sentences are constructed so that they make sense and are grammatically complete. We string words together according to rules we learned as children and refined as adults. The technical terms start to come when we try to describe all the options precisely. The good news is that there are only so many ways of doing this. The bad news is that these ways aren't all straightforward – as Suzie was about to find out.

Interlude: *The first grammarians*

Protagoras

Plato

Aristotle

Priscian

The notion of a sentence-like unit reaches back to the fifth century BC in Greece, where it forms part of the long-running discussions over the best ways of winning a debate – the subject matter of rhetoric. A group of philosophers, known as the Sophists ('wise men'), were fascinated by the way worldly phenomena could be subjected to measurement, and this included language. The best speakers were thought to be those who could come out with carefully crafted utterances of equal length. One of the group, Protagoras, is said to have distinguished different types of sentence, such as statement, question, answer, command, prayer and invitation.

The Greeks didn't have a notion of 'sentence' corresponding to the one we have today. The word for a meaningful utterance, used by Plato, Aristotle, and the group of grammarians known as the Stoics, was *logos* – but its meaning was very broad, including any sort of argument, plan or proposition, as well as structures we would today call sentence, clause, and phrase. Around 100 BC, Dionysius Thrax of Alexandria wrote a short but influential treatise, 'The Art of Grammar' (*Tekhni Grammatiki*), and in one of its sections he described a sentence as a 'complete thought'. Latin writers later took over the idea, especially Priscian in the sixth century AD, which is how it entered European thinking about grammar. His was the standard Latin school textbook, *Institutiones grammaticae* ('Grammatical Foundations'), in the Middle Ages.

It took a millennium for *sentence* to establish itself in English with its present-day grammatical meaning. The modern word comes from Latin *sententia*, but this had the meaning of 'opinion' or 'maxim'. When the Romans wanted to talk about a sentence, they would use *oratio*, which had the same kind of broad meaning as Greek *logos*. So when *sentence* is first recorded in English, in the fourteenth century, it's not surprising to find that it brought its Latin meanings along with it.

We see it used in one of Chaucer's *Canterbury Tales* – 'The Tale of Melibeus'. At one point Dame Prudence asks Melibeus, 'what is your sentence?' She isn't asking about his grammar, but for his opinion about something she's just said. It was a common usage in the Middle Ages. An earlier collection of doctrinal opinions by the Fathers of the Christian Church was called in Latin *Sententiarum libri quatuor*, and this was translated as 'The Four Books of the Sentences'. From there the word developed the meaning of a legal opinion – a decision of a court – and that led to the modern meaning of 'punishment', as in 'a sentence of five years'.

At the same time, the word went in another direction, continuing the meaning of 'pithy saying' or 'maxim'. In Act 1 of Ben Jonson's *Poetaster* (1601), Captain Tucca responds to Ovid, who has been asking a series of succinct pointed questions, by drily commenting: 'Thou speakest sentences.' Again, he isn't commenting on Ovid's grammar, but on his rhetorical ability. However, from there, it is a short step to the modern meaning, which was also well established by the time Jonson was writing. In Shakespeare's *As You Like It* (3.2.132) Orlando pens a love poem, where he promises to write the name of Rosalind 'upon the fairest boughs, / Or at every sentence end'. Evidently, he knows something about grammar.

Second steps: the big picture

Children take their next tentative steps along the grammar road at around eighteen months. They are becoming more active and curious. There is a whole new world to discover. Adults are beginning to talk to them about it. And they want to talk back.

During the first year of life most of the interaction between adult and child is playful. Engaging in a game of peep-bo or round-and-round-the-garden is great fun, but it's hardly a conversation. During the second year, however, the language becomes more serious, with explanations ('That's not a teddy, it's an elephant'), descriptions ('I can see a big red bus'), and warnings ('Don't touch that tap – it's hot'). To adopt an Internet expression: the speech directed to the child now has more content. Adults also start to amplify what toddlers are saying by expanding their holophrases – in effect, showing them how to say more complex things. 'Dog,' says the child. 'Yes, he's a nice big dog,' says the adult. And sooner or later, the child will have a go at the more advanced sentence: 'Big dog.'

What all this interaction does is present the child with example after example of everyday sentences. The utterances are short and to the point. Adults seem to know instinctively just how long to make them. Nobody ever responds to 'Dog' by saying, 'Yes, he's a lovely big dog who barks a lot and who likes to run round the garden chasing a ball.' The result is that children at this age repeatedly hear a set of basic sentence patterns, spoken with a similar rhythm and melody. So it's no surprise that, once they are capable of listening, remembering, and articulating longer sequences of words, these patterns are going to be the ones that characterize their first attempts at more mature sentences.

The period from around eighteen months to two is often called the 'two-word stage', for obvious reasons when we look at this selection of typical sentences. They're all from a child, Victoria, aged twenty-one months:

baby cry	daddy gone	dolly there	gone milk
she drink	drink dolly	it off	that horsie

What's remarkable is that these sentences show she has already mastered the basic principle of grammar: when words come together in a sentence, they perform different roles. We can get a sense of what these roles are if we interpret what she's saying in adult terms, starting with these five:

baby cry	the baby / is crying
daddy gone	daddy / has just gone
dolly there	dolly / is there
gone milk = milk gone	the milk / has just gone
drink dolly = dolly drink	dolly / is drinking

In each sentence she introduces a topic – the name of a someone or a something – building on her earlier ability to name people or objects. Then she says something about it – usually what is happening to it or has just happened to it. In two cases, the action is going on; in two cases the action is over; and in one case she's reporting a location (*there*). It's as if she's getting to grips with the big picture – sketching out a narrative in the broadest terms.

Notice that she's aware of these roles even when she

gets the word order wrong. In English, when you're making a statement, the doer goes before the doing. (It would be the other way round in some languages, such as Welsh.) She knows very well that it's the dolly doing the drinking, and that one can't 'drink dolly'. And if that's so (I imagine her reasoning), then the meaning will come across whatever order the words come out in. Which it does, in this case. It'll be a while before she realizes that changing the word order can change the meaning: *daddy push* is different from *push daddy*.

Grammarians call the names *nouns* and the actions *verbs*. Old grammars would talk about a noun being 'the name of a person, place or thing' – a good start, but not a satisfactory definition, as there are lots of nouns that are none of these, such as those that refer to abstract notions (*conscience, politics, happiness* ...). These grammars would also define verbs as 'doing words' – again, an unsatisfactory definition, as there are many verbs that don't 'do' anything (*is, see, feel* ...). But these definitions do at least capture the way Victoria is thinking of words at this age. She seems to have grasped the principle that words do different jobs in a sentence – and, one far-off day, when in school she starts learning about how to describe the grammar she already speaks, she will find out that these words belong to different 'word classes', traditionally called 'parts of speech'.

Her other sentences show that her rudimentary ideas about grammar aren't restricted to nouns and verbs. She already knows that there are words (such as *she, it,* and *that*) which save you the bother of having to name something a second time.

she drink   *instead of*   dolly drink

In school, she'll learn to call these words *pronouns*. And her early two-word sentences show some other grammatical notions emerging too – but more on that in Chapter 3.

Keywords: subject and predicate

Victoria's insight about the big picture – that sentences can have two parts, each part performing a different role – was also one of the first grammatical insights of the early Greek writers on language. Plato in his *Sophist* (261–2, Harold Fowler's translation) has his Stranger introduce the subject to Theaetetus: 'let us now investigate names', and the dialogue continues:

> Stranger: ... we have two kinds of vocal indications of being.
> Theaetetus: How so?
> Stranger: One called nouns (*onomata*), the other verbs (*rhemata*).
> Theaetetus: Define each of them.
> Stranger: The indication which relates to action we may call a verb.
> Theaetetus: Yes.
> Stranger: And the vocal sign applied to those who perform the actions in question we call a noun.
> Theaetetus: Exactly.
> Stranger: Hence discourse is never composed of nouns alone spoken in succession, nor of verbs spoken without nouns.

To which Theaetetus, perhaps anticipating the twenty-first century, replies:

> Theaetetus: I do not understand that.

and gets a slap on the wrist for not paying attention:

> Stranger: I see; you evidently had something else in mind

when you assented just now; for what I wished to say was
just this, that verbs and nouns do not make discourse if
spoken successively in this way.

But Plato seems to sense that his readers do need an example.

Theaetetus: In what way?
Stranger: For instance, 'walks', 'runs', 'sleeps', and the other
verbs which denote actions, even if you utter all there are of
them in succession, do not make discourse for all that.
Theaetetus: No, of course not.
Stranger: And again, when 'lion', 'stag', 'horse', and all
other names of those who perform these actions are
uttered, such a succession of words does not yet make
discourse; for in neither case do the words uttered indicate
action or inaction or existence of anything that exists or
does not exist, until the verbs are mingled with the nouns;
then the words fit, and their first combination is a sentence,
about the first and shortest form of discourse.

The verbs have to be mingled with the nouns. The Stranger
has, in effect, anticipated the distinction between the one-
word and two-word stages of development in language acquisition. The words in isolation don't 'make a discourse'. Only
by combining them do we make sense.

Translators face a problem with the two critical terms:

rhema – the name of an action (plural *rhemata*)
onoma – the name of the one who performs the action
(plural *onomata*)

To translate them as 'verb' and 'noun' is as near as we can get,
using modern terminology, but Plato's distinction was based
on the meaning of the two parts, and on the way they worked
in sentences to express logical relationships. They aren't

'parts of speech', for that kind of classification of words into classes came later (see Chapter 6).

It took a while for modern grammatical terminology to develop. Eventually, 'the one who performs the action' came to be called the *subject* of the sentence – a natural development of the general meaning of this word – 'subject matter'. Everything else in the sentence was called the *predicate* – a less obvious usage, unless you were familiar with the terms used in logic. So, the sentence *my uncle saw the doctor* would be analysed like this:

My uncle / saw the doctor.
SUBJECT   PREDICATE

That all seems straightforward enough, but in grammar things are never entirely straightforward. This is the Great Truth about grammar: it is an art as well as a science, and it is always possible to analyse sentences in more than one way. Especially when the concepts and terms devised for one language come to be used for another – as here, Greek into English via Latin – there is likely to be scope for different interpretations.

Nobody disagreed about what a subject was. But there were two main differences of opinion about predicates. The first we can see if we look at the kind of sentence used in studies of logic:

My uncle is a doctor.

Logicians would say that *a doctor* is the predicate – that which is said of the subject. They would ignore the verb *is*, as they saw its function to be simply a way of linking the subject to the predicate. They called this verb the *copula* (from a Latin word meaning 'fasten together' – and yes, it is the same root as in *copulate*). If the job of the copula was to link the two parts of the sentence, then it couldn't be part of either.

This is how the term *predicate* was used when it arrived in English in the fifteenth century as part of the study of logic. But a century later, when grammarians began to analyse English sentences, a problem arose:

- Some continued to think that the copula wasn't part of the predicate, on the grounds that it had no meaning. They seemed to think of the sentence as if it were 'my uncle – doctor'. This wouldn't be grammatical in English (though it would in Russian), but it expresses the same meaning.
- Others disagreed. They thought the copula *was* part of the predicate, on the grounds that it was a verb, acting like any other verb – for example, able to change its tense:

  A. My uncle / knows a doctor. My uncle / knew a doctor.
  B. My uncle / is a doctor.   My uncle / was a doctor.

If the subject/predicate division is made after the word *uncle* in the A pair of sentences, it was argued, why not in the B pair? This is the way these sentences are usually analysed nowadays, but the question of where to start the predicate caused a lot of heart-searching among early grammarians of English.

That wasn't the only issue. What to do with longer sentences like this one?

My uncle saw the doctor yesterday in London.

The question here was what to do with the extra bits. *Yesterday* and *in London* could be omitted from the sentence and the sentence would still make sense. Grammarians began to call them *adjuncts* (from a Latin word meaning 'associated' or 'relevant'). So, how should a grammarian deal with adjuncts? Were they part of the predicate or not? Once again, there were two options.

- Some thought the adjuncts were part of the predicate, on the grounds that their job was to amplify the meaning of the verb – when did the action of seeing take place? Where did it take place? They would analyse the sentence like this:

My uncle / saw the doctor yesterday in London.
SUBJECT   PREDICATE

Just as adjectives say more about nouns, they argued – as in *young doctor* – so adjuncts say more about verbs – *see yesterday*.

- Others disagreed. They thought adjuncts shouldn't be part of the predicate, on the grounds that they weren't essential to the core meaning of what's being said – that an uncle is seeing a doctor, regardless of when or where. So they would analyse the sentence like this:

My uncle / saw the doctor / yesterday in London.
SUBJECT   PREDICATE   ADJUNCTS

You'll find both these views represented in grammar books today – as well as a third: that it's better to avoid the term *predicate* altogether, on the grounds that it's too broad a notion. There are so many kinds of construction in English that can be grouped under the heading of predicate – this view argues – that it makes more sense to study these constructions directly. I'll talk about what these are in Chapter 8, but it's worth noting now that, despite its long history in English language study, some grammars today don't mention the word *predicate* at all.

Now, if you're already asking 'but which of these different views is correct?' you're not thinking like a modern grammarian. The point is that there's a good reason to support each analysis; and what makes grammar interesting – at least, to grammarians – is evaluating the arguments that support one view rather than another. Some of these arguments are scientific in character, based on an assessment of the consequences that follow from taking a particular view. But – and this is the point that's often forgotten – some are aesthetic arguments: one analysis is thought to be 'simpler' or 'more satisfying' or 'more elegant' than another. This isn't an issue found only in grammar, of course. Biologist Peter Medawar called his influential philosophical account of scientific method *The Art of the Soluble* (1968).

It's this insight that is often forgotten by those in ministries of education around the world who think that grammar can be tested in the same way as spelling or mathematics. Schools have to teach a standard, of course, and children have to learn that standard, if their spoken and written usage is to live up to the expectations of society. Testing is a way of trying to make that happen. But it should never be forgotten that the usages that make up this standard, and the ways in which these are analysed and described, comprise a selection from a set of practices and opinions that are at times diverse. The challenge, as I'll discuss in Chapter 25, is to find ways of testing grammar that either avoid the diversity or, better, build it into the educational system.

3
Second steps: the small picture

Victoria, of course, is oblivious of all the issues to do with what a predicate is or isn't. As far as she's concerned, a sentence simply has two parts, and that's enough. But actually, the way she puts the two parts together shows that she's already combining them in several different ways. As well as the kinds of 'big picture' sentence we saw her using in Chapter 2, we see examples like these, where she seems to be homing in on details – the 'small picture':

my bed   silly hat   more toy   my apple   hat mummy

These are all cases where a noun has been given a more specific focus compared with what she was able to say during her holophrastic stage. Not just any old bed, but *my bed*. Not just any old hat, but a *silly hat*. These sentences show that she's already learned another basic principle of grammar: that some words can be subordinate to other words, sharpening their meaning – making it more particular. Grammarians talk about one word *modifying* another or *qualifying* another.

Suzie was doing the same thing, at this age. Her vocabulary wasn't exactly the same as Victoria's, but she could say such things as:

my car
big car
more car

She was clearly beginning to think of cars in more particular ways. She said *my car* when her older brother tried to take a toy car away from her: mine, not yours! She said *big car* after she was asked whether she wanted a big car or a little one. She said *more car* after putting six toy cars into a box and finding there was room for others. By themselves, *my* or *big* or *more* have an uncertain meaning – these are the holophrases of Chapter 1. But, used along with *car*, they give the sentences a new life. Each one is a new story.

When words are used in this way – one depending on the other and sharpening its meaning – grammarians call the construction a *phrase*. And because *car* is a noun, they would call Suzie's utterances *noun phrases*. *Car* is said to be the *head* – the chief word – of the noun phrase. Later, she'll learn that there are other kinds of phrase, and I'll talk about those in Chapter 4. But all phrases do the same job: they convey small pictures.

These sharply focusing words – *my, silly, more, mummy* – are of various kinds. When Victoria and Suzie start using them in more advanced sentences, they will learn that they function in very different ways. Words like *silly* they will come to call *adjectives*, and they'll discover that they can do wonderful things with them, such as comparing. That hat is *silly*, but that one is *sillier* – and that one is *silliest* of all! This is an exciting discovery – a taste of the glamour that is hidden within every grammatical construction.

The girls have the order of the words right too – *my bed*, not *bed my*; *more toy*, not *toy more*. But *hat mummy* seems to have gone wrong: Victoria meant *mummy's hat*. She'll have to work on that – and in the process learn one of the less straightforward things about English grammar – that some possessing words need *'s* endings and others (such as *my*) don't. She'll also find that she can't play comparing games with nouns like *mummy*: she won't normally hear people saying that one mummy is *mummier* than another.

This is part of the girls' grammatical future, and it will take them quite some time to work out all the ways in which these words can or can't be used. In the meantime, both of them spent much of the six months up to the age of two consolidating their basic grammatical skills. Their vocabulary was also growing rapidly – by two, around 200 words – and they put these new words to work in the familiar sentence frames: *see birdie, see elephant, see fairy … my elephant, my ball, my socks …* Recordings show them using hundreds of two-word sentences – some big picture, some small picture. And with all this new vocabulary, the stage is set for them to take on board another major grammatical principle – but that's for the next chapter.

Keyword: syntax

With hardly any exceptions, the two-word sentences in this chapter and the previous one show the girls beginning to respect the principle of word order. In English, the order of words is crucial to producing sentences that we can understand. Adults know that *the dog is chasing the cat* makes sense whereas *dog is cat the chasing* does not. They also know that changing the word order can alter the sense of a sentence in quite fundamental ways. *The dog is chasing the cat* is by no means the same as *the cat is chasing the dog*, nor is *the taxi is here* the same as *is the taxi here*, or *I had my hair washed* the same as *I had washed my hair*.

The chief characteristic of English grammar is the way words are arranged within sentences, and the technical term for this process is *syntax*. It is, yet again, a term derived from Greek, where *syntaksis* meant 'orderly arrangement' – of anything. It became part of grammar, in a more restricted sense, after Priscian used it in his Latin textbook to talk about word order, and that is the usage that arrived in English, via French, in the sixteenth century. It came to be seen as a major part of grammar. Ben Jonson, writing in the early 1600s, begins his *English Grammar* in this way:

> Grammar is the art of true and well-speaking a language;

and he immediately divides the subject into two parts:

> Etymology – the true notation of words
> Syntax – the right ordering of them

But the original, more general sense of *syntax* wasn't forgotten. Over the centuries it was used to describe such domains as the distribution of plants in a garden, the arrangement of elements in a musical composition ('musical syntax'), the connection between the bones of the body, and the organization of items in a recipe. It still generates such general applications. It is a central notion in programming computers. The *Oxford English Dictionary* (*OED*) has a citation from 2011 in which a writer talks about 'the syntax of the comic strip'. And I once saw in a shop window (in Soho, London) a book called *The Syntax of Sex*.

Back in the world of grammar, you might think that the next step would be to explore the arrangement of the words in a sentence. Does the subject go before the predicate or the other way round? If there are several words in the predicate, what order should they be in? But there is something that has to be in place before these questions can be answered, and Suzie homes in on it as she enters her third year.

4
Third steps: combining big and small

String the words together, in the right order. That seems to be Suzie's first grammatical principle. And it works well enough as long as she's saying simple sentences such as *red car* and *car gone*. But there comes a point – and it usually happens around age two – when children are more ambitious, wanting to combine the big picture and the small picture by saying such things as *red car gone*.

This is quite a step forward, because sentences like that are doing something new. It's no longer just a matter of stringing words together. There are *levels* of structure in the sentence now: the small picture is inside the big one. You can see the two levels of structure if the sentence is drawn like this:

```
car          gone
 /\
red car
```

Red goes with *car* and not with *gone*. It would be a curious sort of error for Suzie to say *red gone*. She'll certainly never hear her caretakers saying something like that.

Once she got the idea, she started to fill out lots of her sentences in this way. *See car* and *red car* became *see red car*. *Where hat?* and *silly hat* became *where silly hat?* In each case a noun phrase became part of a larger sentence. Hundreds of new sentences of this kind appeared as she passed her second birthday – too many for me to record.

During her two-word period, Suzie had also begun to experiment with other sorts of phrase. She seemed to realize that words like *silly* could also be modified: *very silly*. *Silly* is the word whose meaning is now being sharpened, and because *silly* is an adjective grammarians would call this an *adjective phrase*. And it wasn't long before this phrase too was incorporated into a bigger sentence: *there very silly hat*. An ambitious four-worder!

Verbs started to get the same treatment. She began to focus on actions, copying the way her parents talked when describing pictures in a book, saying things like *The duck is swimming in the pond, The bear's hiding in his cave,* and *The little girl is eating an ice cream.* In due course, Suzie came out with *is eating* – sometimes with the word-ending, sometimes without it: *is eat*. *Eat* is the word whose meaning is now being sharpened, and because *eat* is a verb, it could be called a *verb phrase*. (But beware: some grammarians, such as Noam Chomsky, use *verb phrase* in a much wider sense, equivalent to the *predicate* of traditional grammars.)

It took a while before Suzie worked out what that 'little word' *is* actually does in the verb phrase. Its meaning isn't as clear-cut as *little* or *very*. She sensed that a word needed to be there, but she often made the wrong choice, for at various times she said *girl am eating, girl do eat,* and *girl be eating.* Later, she'd learn that these little words are also verbs, and have different meanings, but they belong to a group of a very special kind. Their job is to convey different ways of viewing the action expressed by the main verb. People sometimes describe them as 'helping' verbs – modern grammars usually call them *auxiliary verbs*.

And she began to use another kind of phrase, especially to express location. She said such things as *in car* and *on chair,* and then put these into bigger sentences: *go in car, dolly on chair.*

The critical words in these expressions are the prepositions *in* and *on*. These are words that 'pre-pose' (are placed before) other words to show a relationship of some kind – in this case, the location of the car and the chair. Grammarians thus came to call constructions of this kind *prepositional phrases*.

Then Suzie made another small but significant step forward. If you can put one phrase into a bigger sentence, then why not two? So we get the following:

It may be a small step, but it suddenly made her sentence look impressively mature.

Keyword: phrase

Phrase comes from Greek *phrasis*, which had a range of very general senses. It usually meant a way of speaking or a characteristic style of expression, and this is how it first came into English, via Latin, in the sixteenth century. Echoes of this old use are still heard today, when we talk of 'a turn of phrase' or comment on someone's 'phrasing', or use a 'phrase book' to interpret expressions in a foreign language.

In the second half of the seventeenth century, when the first school grammars of English were written, *phrase* began to be used more narrowly, but it still kept its general meaning. Bishop Lowth, in his *Short Introduction to English Grammar* (1762), gives a typical definition:

> A phrase is two or more words rightly put together, in order to make a part of a sentence; and sometimes making a whole sentence.

In effect, he's saying you can use this term to describe more or less any string of words you want to talk about!

This vague state of affairs couldn't continue. As grammars became more detailed, writers needed to find more precise ways of describing the clusters of words that form a part of a sentence. They noted that these clusters had a unity of their own, and that their construction was very different from the overall structure of a sentence. As we saw in Chapter 2, sentences had two parts, a subject and a predicate; but these new clusters seemed to have no such structure. Either they lacked a predicate:

> a silly hat
> in the garden
> a boy on a bicycle

or they lacked a subject:

> is eating
> has been moved

How were these to be described?

It took over 200 years to produce a reasonably comprehensive description of the way phrases are constructed in English, and the linguistic journals still have articles debating the best way of analysing some of their features. The reason is that they are so diverse and extendable, and their meanings are often very tricky to explain.

You can get a sense of the complexity by building up a noun phrase of your own. You can start by adding words before the head noun:

> hats
> the hats
> the silly hats

the silly red clown hat
all the silly red clown hats
not quite almost all of the silly red clown hats

and then add words after the head noun:

hats on the hatstand
hats on the hatstand worn by the children
hats on the hatstand that I knitted last week

(And yes, this feature allows for all sorts of jokes and ambiguities, such as knitted hatstands.) Several of these features could be continued indefinitely. There's no theoretical limit to the number of adjectives you can have before a noun:

the silly, ugly, fashionable, expensive, comfortable ...

or the number of prepositional phrases you can have after it:

... on the hatstand, in different colours, with ribbons, from France ...

The grammatical devil lies in the detail. It may seem the most natural thing in the world to string adjectives and adjective-like words together, such as *the silly red clown hats*. We don't think twice about it. But few people realize the complexity of what they're doing, for the ordering of these words is something they have had to learn. To take just one feature: we cannot say *the clown silly red hats* or *the red clown silly hats*. Why not? It's not at all easy to work out the rules governing our usage here.

When sentences start to look complicated, it's usually because they contain a lot of phrases, each one of which has a structure of its own. This is the danger. If you're new to grammar work, what you must never do is allow yourself to be distracted at the outset by all the phrase-level detail.

The first step is to see that these sentences, at a higher level, usually have a basic and simple structure. You have to hang on to that, otherwise you'll drown.

So, faced with a monster like this:

> All the people who voted in favour of reform in the recent ballot are expecting a serious revision of the rules governing voting procedure.

the critical thing is to spell out that basic structure:

> people expect revision

Then everything else falls into place:

> what kind of people? all those who voted ...
> what kind of revision? a serious one of the rules ...

Suzie wasn't presented with sentences as complicated as that; but the ones she did hear from her parents gave her the same kind of problem. Here was one sentence she heard from her mother at tidying-up time:

> Those dollies need to go in the cupboard.

She too had to disregard the detail and find that basic structure.

> dollies go cupboard

This is the task to which she devoted a great deal of her linguistic energy, between two and three years of age, and I'll describe how she did it in Chapter 6. But before moving on to that more advanced stage, there's one more thing to notice in her two-year-old sentences. She has added a third level to her grammatical repertoire.

5

Inside the words

Talking about her favourite doll, Suzie said such things as *dolly chair*. And when that doll joined her friends in a toy car, she said *dollies in car*. At a birthday party, she was able to name several of the coloured paper hats. She told us that hers was a *red hat* and that her friend Joanne had a *blue hat*. And then, when other children arrived and started to dress up, she said *more hats*. She had learned the crucial difference between 'one' and 'more than one', which grammars describe as the contrast between singular and plural.

In English, the easiest way of understanding how to make this contrast is to take a singular noun and 'add an *s*'. So we have *cats, dogs,* and *horses*. It's a nice simple rule when we're writing these words down. But when speaking them, that -*s* hides something more complex, as three different pronunciations are involved. If the vocal cords are buzzing at the end of the noun, the -*s* sounds like a -*z*: *dogs, cars, bees, dreams*. If they aren't, it sounds like a -*ss*: *cats, cups, socks, coughs*. And if the final consonant is already like an -*s* or -*z*, an extra syllable is added: *horses, quizzes, dishes, bridges*.

Those phonetic differences are quite subtle, but by age two Suzie could say all three word-endings correctly: *cats, dogs, horses*. And she discovered that other words had endings too. *Running* appeared alongside *run; biggest* alongside *big; jumped* alongside *jump*. During her third year she began to learn her next big principle of grammar: that you can express meanings not just by changing the order of words in a sentence, but by changing the way a word is formed.

It's a third level, as can be seen if we extend the kind of diagram I used in Chapter 4:

When Suzie says *red cars gone*, she's doing three grammatical things at once – a multitasking ability that is at the heart of grammar.

She doesn't know it, but her word-level task in learning English is not going to be very great. English has very few word-endings that make a grammatical contrast – fewer than a dozen. As well as adding an *-s* to make a plural, she will learn that *-s* can also be used with many nouns to express possession, as in *mummy's bag*. And *-s* can be used with verbs too, as in *he sees*. She'll find out that if you add an *-ed* ending onto a verb, it changes the time frame, either to the distant past (as in *I jumped*) or the recent past (as in *I have jumped*). She'll learn the two adjective endings that express degrees of comparison, as in *bigger* and *biggest*. She'll discover that some pronouns change their form, such as *he* becoming *him*, depending on where it's used in a sentence. And she'll learn that you can shorten some words and use them as word-endings, such as *isn't* from *is not* and *he's* from *he is*.

It didn't take Suzie long to acquire these word-endings. She would be using all of them by her third birthday. Her task wasn't over, as she still had to learn that English has quite a few irregular ways of making plurals (such as *mice*, not *mouses*) and past forms of verbs (such as *took*, not *taked*).

Word-sets such as *I, me, my*, and *mine* would also cause a few problems. I'll talk about those in Chapter 6. But her main work at the third level was done.

Of course, if she had been learning Spanish or French, where there are far more word-endings, her task would have taken much longer. Some languages, such as Latin, have hundreds of endings. Several African languages have thousands. A Finnish Suzie has to learn that there are as many as fifteen endings on nouns, expressing the different kinds of meaning that in English are expressed by such prepositions as *in* and *on*. So it will take a Finnish child much longer to learn word-endings than an English child. On the other hand, an English child has much more to learn about the use of prepositions.

All children end up speaking their own language by more or less the same age, regardless of where the grammatical complexity lies. If a language expresses meanings using lots of word-endings, it doesn't need to use word order so much to do the job. And vice versa. There's a British idiom that captures this balance nicely, originating in the way fairground owners think about their daily profits: what you lose on the swings you gain on the roundabouts. As all English learners discover, they have a challenging time when it comes to the syntactic swings; but life gets a lot easier when it comes to the morphological roundabouts.

Keyword: morphology

Knowing about word-endings explains a lot about the character of the first English grammars, which began to appear towards the end of the sixteenth century. The writers simply copied the way their classical predecessors had described the grammar of Latin, and later grammarians followed their lead, right into the twentieth century. These were the unglamorous centuries. They failed to take into account that the way English grammar worked was very different from the way Latin grammar worked.

We're still trying to get rid of the pernicious influence of Latin on the way we think about English grammar. Several of the worries people have about 'correct' usage are the consequence of being conditioned to think about English as if it were Latin. If you've ever been uncertain about *it is me/I* or *between you and me/I*, or worried about whether you should split an infinitive or end a sentence with a preposition, then you've been led into the Latin trap – a process that, for centuries, began in school. I'll talk more about these usage issues in Chapter 12.

As a result, you can't understand the way the study of English grammar developed, with all its off-putting terminology, if you don't know something about the classical background, and in particular about the way Latin grammar worked. As I said in my introduction, grammar exists to make sense of words. In English, we do this primarily through varying our word order – syntax. In Latin, they did it primarily through varying their word-endings – morphology. This is a huge difference, but people had to wait for the emergence of modern linguistic science in order to appreciate it.

The term *morphology* arrived in the early nineteenth century as part of the explosive development of scientific enquiry. In biology, people talked about the morphology of plants; in physiology, about the morphology of cells; in geology, about the morphology of hills and mountains. The common theme was the study of structure – the parts of an entity and their relationships. Linguists applied the term to the study of the structure of words, and in particular to the word-beginnings and word-endings that express grammatical relationships.

Morphology replaced an earlier term that described the

way the endings of a word varied: *accidence*. That name had come about because early Latin grammarians thought of these variations as 'accidents' (Latin *accidentia*) – forms that weren't essential to a word's identity. It went out of favour when linguists in the 1930s began to report the extraordinary diversity in word structure among the languages of the world. They felt that the highly complex structure of words in, for example, American Indian languages – where grammatical relationships were expressed not only by word-endings (suffixes) but also by word-beginnings (prefixes) and word-middles (infixes) – wasn't well captured by a term that had hitherto been primarily used just for word-endings. They saw *morphology* as a more inclusive term – and moreover one that suggested a new direction in linguistic study, where the unique grammatical character of every language was to be respected.

They did, however, keep the term *inflection* (also spelled *inflexion*) to refer to the actual forms that conveyed these relationships. This derives from Latin *inflexio*, related to the verb *flectere* meaning 'to bend'. As with many grammatical terms, the same word is found in other areas of study, such as optics (the bending of a ray of light) and geometry (the point where a curve changes from convex to concave, or vice versa). In grammar, an inflection was seen as a word 'bending' in different directions, depending on the meaning to be expressed. So in the study of English grammar, you will see the word-endings described as *inflections*, or sometimes (to make it clear which part of the word is involved) *inflectional endings*.

The early writers on English grammar didn't just take over the terms: they adopted the entire approach to classification used by the Latin grammarians, notably Varro and Priscian. The Latin writers didn't always agree on points of detail – for example, which form of a word to take as the 'basic' form (the one you would list as the headword in a dictionary) – but they saw real merit in grouping these forms into tables, so that all the forms of a noun went together, all the forms of a verb, and so on. Apart from anything else, they saw this as a convenient method of teaching Latin to foreigners – a major task in an expanding European empire. And when Latin became the default language of learning and education, in medieval Europe, a version of these tables, with all their associated nomenclature, became the pedagogical norm.

Ever since, schoolchildren have learned Latin starting with the word-endings on verbs and nouns, to the extent that *amo, amas, amat* – the equivalents of 'I love', 'you (singular) love', and 'he, she, it loves' – have attained a recognition value well beyond their original standing. Harry Mount called his successful introduction to Latin (2006) *Amo, Amas, Amat ... and All That*. It was an approach that captured well the totally morphological character of the language, but it presented a steep learning curve for English speakers, unused to such word complexity. I well remember, in my early teens, the hours spent assimilating the 100+ endings to enable me to express all tenses, persons, numbers, and moods of loving – *amabo* 'I will love', *amavi* 'I have loved' – and then discovering that not all verbs used the same word-endings. And then taking on board the technical term, derived from Latin, for these different sets of verb endings: *conjugations*. I learned to *conjugate* a verb – rattle off all the correct word-endings, and say what they mean. Later I learned that this term has the same basic meaning (of 'connection' or 'combination') seen in *conjugal*.

At the same time, I learned that nouns, adjectives and pronouns also had sets of word-endings, called *cases*, each expressing a grammatical relationship. *Case* comes from *casus* in Latin, which had a wide range of meanings, such as 'fall' and 'accident'; so in using this word to describe nouns, grammarians seem to have thought of the different forms of a noun as 'falling away' from the basic form. As with verbs, the noun inflections were organized into tables, and these too had to be painstakingly learned. I remember calling these noun tables *conjugations*, and being told off because they were *declensions*. It's an interesting usage: the original sense of *decline* was 'turn aside' or 'deviate' from a norm of some kind – as when we talk of someone's health declining. In grammar, the different cases were evidently thought of as departures from the basic form. Here are examples for the noun *friend*.

- If you wanted to convey that a noun was the doer of an action, as in *My <u>friend</u> visited me*, you would use the *nominative* case, *amicus* – the 'naming' case. Nouns used in this way would act as the subject in a sentence (see Chapter 2). Words that stood for nouns (as in <u>He</u> *visited*) or depended on them (as in <u>My</u> *friend*) would also be in the nominative case.

- If you wanted to address the noun, as in *Lovely to see you, my <u>friend</u>*, you would use the *vocative* case, *amice* – the 'calling' case. Latin vocatives would usually be translated into English using *O* (*O friend!*), and this led to one of the more bizarre practices in early English grammar teaching, when students would solemnly have to learn every case for all nouns. I remember textbooks presenting me with such phrases as 'O table' and 'O stone', and wondering how such a situation could ever arise.

- If you wanted to show that the noun was directly affected by an action, as in *I visited my <u>friend</u>*, you would use the *accusative* case, *amicum*. Nouns in the accusative case would act as the object of a verb in a sentence. The term was opaque, as it has nothing to do with 'accusing'. Its origin lies in a remarkable instance of misinterpretation. The Greek grammarians used the word *aitiatikos* (from *aitia*, which meant 'cause, reason') to describe the case of a noun used in this way. Latin grammarians – evidently not being as good at Greek as they should have been – took this word to be from the similar-sounding *aitiasthai*, meaning 'find fault, censure', and translated it as *accusativus*, and this is how it was turned into English when words were used as the object of a verb. Linguists, anxious to get away from the Latin associations of the word, usually replace *accusative* by *objective* when describing English. So, when pronouns are used as the object of a verb, and change their form, such as *he* becoming *him* and *we* becoming *us*, the *him/us* forms are said to be in the *objective case*.

• If you wanted to convey that the noun was the possessor or source of something, as in *My friend's car*, you would use the *genitive* case, *amici* – another opaque term, as it does not mean 'relating to the generation of offspring' (as in the 'genitive organs', or genitals). Here too, the Greek grammatical term was misunderstood by the Latin grammarians, who thought that *geniki*, meaning 'generic', was indeed something to do with human generation, for which their word was *genetivus*. Varro actually called it the *patricus casus*, the 'fatherly case'. Modern linguists often replace it by the more transparent *possessive case*.

• If you wanted to show that the noun was indirectly affected by an action, as in *I gave the book to my friend*, you would use the *dative* case, *amico* – the 'giving' case, usually expressed in English using the prepositions *to* or *for*, or (without the preposition) by word order (*I gave my friend the book*). The word is a straightforward translation from the Greek verb meaning 'to give', which in Latin was *dare*, 'to give'. *Data* (singular *datum*) is a related word: items of information that have been collected or 'given'.

- If you wanted to show that the noun was the manner or means by which an action is performed, as in *I learned the news through my friend*, you would use the *ablative* case, *amico* – usually expressed in English using the prepositions *by*, *with*, or *from*. The Latin word *ablativus* literally meant 'relating to the action of taking away'. The modern surgical term *ablation* echoes this, and there are echoes in aero science too. When space scientists talk about *ablative materials*, they're referring to ways of protecting the surface of space vehicles, not techniques for teaching astronauts Latin.

This is just half the story, of course, for every one of these cases also had a plural form. Indeed, it is far less than half, for only a proportion of the nouns in Latin had endings like those in *amicus*. There were five declensions of Latin nouns, each with its own set of inflections, as well as many exceptions. It all added up to a language that was totally morphology-driven, very different from English, but one whose economy of expression, powerful oratorical rhythms, stylistic diversity, and literary brilliance gave it unparalleled status in medieval Europe as a model of linguistic excellence. If the English language could live up to its standards, English grammarians felt, it would be doing very well.

Interlude: The first English grammarian

William Bullokar (c. 1531–1609) was one of the first spelling reformers, devising a 40-letter phonetic alphabet for English, which he used in a 68-page *Pamphlet for Grammar*, published in 1586 – the first known attempt to write an English grammar. This is how he introduces his book (I've modernized the spelling):

> William Bullokar's Pamphlet for Grammar: Or rather to be said his abbreviation of his Grammar for English, extracted out of his Grammar at Large. This being sufficient for the speedy learning of how to parse English speech for the perfecter writing thereof, and using the best phrase therein; and the easier entrance into the secrets of grammar for other languages, and the speedier understanding of other languages, ruled or not ruled by grammar; very profitable for the English nation that desireth to learn any strange language, and very aidful to the stranger to learn English perfectly and speedily; for that English hath short rule (therefore soon learned) yet having sufficient rules therein to make the way much easier for the learning of any other language unknown before to the learner.

Unfortunately, the *Grammar at Large* has not survived, so all we have is this outline, partly written in jaunty four-line rhyming verses. But it's enough to show his total dependence on Latin grammar in organizing his thinking about English. After an exposition in prose, he ends his booklet with a set of rhyming verses, and his heading shows his mindset:

> Brief notes in verse for parsing English in
> many points agreeing with
> Latin as followeth.

Bꝛef notꝫ in vers foꝛ parcing engliſh in many poyntꝫ agreing with latin aꝫ foloweth.

Firſt mark the partꝫ of ſpech of woꝛdꝫ
   in euery ſentenc,
Noting ſynꝫ and eqiuocalꝫ
   too ynderſtand their ſenc.
Then not æch verbꝫ nominatiu,
   ſett moſt befoꝛ the verb,
Except the verb aſk qeſtion,
   oꝛ be the bidẏng mꝏd.

The opening of William Bullokar's metrical exposition

First mark the parts of speech of words
   in every sentence,
Noting signs and equivocals
   to understand their sense.
Then note each verb's nominative
   set most before the verb,
Except the verb ask question
   or be the bidding mood …

His terminology is taken straight out of Latin grammars, especially the one written by William Lily, with just a few exceptions. (*Equivocal* was one: this was his term for a word that could be used as different parts of speech – he gives the example of *but*, which can be used as a noun or verb (modern spelling, *butt*) or as a conjunction.) The extract also shows an early use of the verb *parse*, meaning to analyse a sentence into its component parts, assigning each word to a part of speech.

This was the beginning of a Latin approach to English grammar that lasted until well into the twentieth century. An example is J. C. Nesfield's *English Grammar* (1898), which was still being reprinted in the 1960s: he accepts that the term *case* is 'inappropriate', because nouns don't change their form apart from the possessive, but he can't rid himself of the old mindset, and nonetheless lists them, as in this chapter, having nominative, vocative, accusative, genitive and dative cases.

6
Talking about mouses

When Suzie realized she could talk about lots of things just by 'adding an s', as in *cats, dogs,* and *horses,* I can imagine her feeling that this grammar business was easy. Certainly she lost no time in applying that *-s* to all kinds of nouns – *cars, buses, dollies, prams, flowers* – and then, one day, *mouses. Me not like them mouses,* she said, when she was about two and a half.

Like everyone who learns a new language, she was working on the assumption that the rules work all the time. The grim reality is that no inflectional language works like that. There are always exceptions – irregular forms. They are the bane of every language learner's existence. I spent I don't know how many hours learning Latin irregular verbs, and then having to do the same thing all over again with French. English learners face the same difficulty.

The problem is greater for verbs than for nouns. There are only a few dozen nouns that have unpredictable plurals – words like *mice, geese, teeth, men, feet, women, cacti* (alongside *cactuses*), and *children* – where the forms simply have to be learned by heart. But there are over 250 irregular verbs, where the simple rule 'add *-ed* to make a past form', as in *I walk* becomes *I walked,* doesn't apply. *I take* becomes *I took. I am* becomes *I was. I say* becomes *I said. I go* becomes *I went.*

Suzie, of course, happily ignored these exceptions when she first encountered the words. So we heard *mouses* and *mans* as well as *taked* and *goed.* Then, as it dawned on her that grown-ups were saying something different, she tried out *mices* and *mens*, along with *tooked* and *wented*. Eventually, *mice*, *men*, *took*, and *went* triumphed. But it took her a long time to work out all the irregular forms. She had most of them sorted by the time she was four, but occasional uncertainties continued well into primary school. She was still coming out with *tooken* when she was nine, especially when she was tired. Maybe she still does.

Actually, uncertainties over irregular forms are never completely resolved. That's one of the sources of usage controversies. Is it *I highlighted the words* or *I highlit the words? Sped* or *speeded? Spelt* or *spelled? Swam* or *swum?* One of the factors is that forms vary somewhat around the regional dialects of English. Brits say *dived*; Americans also say *dove*. In many parts of England, gardeners talk about the way weeds *sprung up*, not *sprang up*. I heard someone on a television gardening programme talk about how he had *strum* the edges of his lawn, not *strimmed*. Where I live, in North Wales, people sometimes say *jamp* for *jumped*.

Why do irregular forms exist? Why don't the rules work all the time? The answer must lie deep within the history of a language, but it's an unattainable answer. Nobody really knows why, when languages were in their earliest state, the speakers treated words in different ways. It must have been something to do with how they felt that some words had something in common – male words vs female words, animate entities vs inanimate entities, slow actions vs sudden actions, and the like. Or perhaps it was simply the fact that one word sounded like another that caused them to be treated in the same way. Then, over long periods of time, the groupings changed, so that, by the time a language came to be written down, we see only remnants of the original system.

We know that many different factors were involved

because we see them at work in the historical texts of a language, and can observe them still operating. When English was first recorded, in Anglo-Saxon times, there were far more word-endings and irregular forms than are found today. Old English was a strongly inflected language – closer to the system we find in Latin, in fact, than to what we have now. A noun like *cyning*, 'king', had not only a genitive form, similar to today (*cyninges*), but also a dative form (*cyninge*); and all forms changed when used in the plural (*cyningas, cyninga, cyningum*). The history of English grammar shows the way these endings gradually ceased to be used, with just a few traces of the original system remaining (such as the possessive case in nouns). Some irregular forms became regular over the centuries: we say *helped* and *dared* now, but in Shakespeare's day it was *holp* and *durst*. And some new irregular forms have arisen: we say *dug* and *caught* now, but we see *digged* and *catched* in Shakespeare. In living memory we have seen *broadcasted* become *broadcast,* presumably following the pattern of *cast* and *forecast*.

Grammar historians spend many happy hours trying to find explanations for why one word moves in direction A while another moves in direction B. But for a language learner such as Suzie, all this is beside the point. All she wants to do is copy the usage she hears around her. She'll learn about the explanations and complications arising out of language change when she gets to school.

Keywords: parts of speech (word classes)

Putting words into groups governed the way the Greek and Roman grammarians thought about language. With a highly inflected language, this was the obvious thing to do. It was logical – and good teaching practice – to put all the words that used the same set of endings into a single class. The English grammarians adopted the idea, calling each class a *part of speech.*

Why 'part of *speech*'? Nouns, verbs, and the other classes all appear in writing as well, so the term is somewhat misleading. It's another example of a poor translation. Dionysius Thrax is the first writer we know to talk about word classes as a whole: he called them *meros logou* – 'part of a sentence/ clause/phrase' (*logou* is the genitive case of *logos*, which, as we saw in Chapter 1, was a very broad term). Priscian, following the Greek tradition, translated the expression as *partes orationis, oratio* having the same kind of broad meaning as *logos*. But *oratio* in Latin also had the meaning of 'speech', and when the word arrived in English as *oration*, in the fifteenth century, that was the sense in which everyone came to know it. As a result, when English grammars came to be written, they translated *partes orationis* as 'parts of speech'.

In modern approaches to grammar, the term *parts of speech* has generally been replaced by *word classes*, for two reasons. The obvious one is to get away from the misleading suggestion that these notions are relevant only for speech. Less obviously, it's to get away from the Latin tradition that makes everyone think that there's a fixed and limited number of word classes in a language – eight or nine – and that these are found in every language. In fact, word classes vary greatly across the languages of the world, and it often proves useful to identify a group of words with a particular grammatical function that has no counterpart in Latin grammar.

It took several centuries to develop the modern system of word classes. Plato, as we saw in Chapter 2, introduced the basic distinction between (what would later be called) nouns and verbs. Aristotle added a third class of words that he called *syndesmoi* – a ragbag of items that were neither nouns nor verbs, such as conjunctions and the definite article. It was a very primitive account, but it motivated the Stoic grammarians, beginning in the third century BC, to develop the system of word classes into the form that has come down to us today.

They first separated the non-noun/non-verb forms that were inflected (what would later be called the pronouns and – in Greek – the articles) from the forms that didn't vary (what would later be called the prepositions and conjunctions). They divided nouns into two types: proper (as in *Athens*) and common (as in *city*). And they distinguished a group of words that seemed to fall between verbs and nouns – what would later be called adverbs. This is the basis of the system that appears in the earliest surviving work on Greek grammar, by Dionysius Thrax (see p. 8), who increased the number of classes to eight, glossed here with English examples:

- noun, combining common and proper (and including adjectives): *Athens, city*
- verb: *go*
- participle, sharing features of both noun and verb: *smoking*
- adverb: *slowly*
- conjunction: *and*
- preposition: *in*
- article: *the*
- pronoun: *I*

This was the work that influenced all subsequent grammars, first in Latin, and eventually in English.

The number of classes recognized has changed over the centuries. Thrax's eight classes became seven in Latin, because there was no separate article word in that language, and then became eight again when writers added a class for interjections (words that expressed an emotion, such as *Oh!*).

The first Latin grammars by English authors – such as the one written by Abbot Ælfric in the eleventh century – follow Priscian's approach exactly, and we see this tradition continuing into the sixteenth century in the widely used school grammar by William Lily. No surprise, then, that it appears in the first English grammars by William Bullokar (p. 38) and dramatist Ben Jonson. Even though the articles *a*(*n*) and *the* are such an important feature of English, the Latin mindset ruled, and they are given no separate mention.

It may surprise a modern reader to see that these writers don't treat adjectives as a separate class. This is because the Latin grammarians saw adjectives as falling within the class of nouns, as for the most part they shared the same inflections. Ben Jonson does the same thing, dividing his class of nouns into substantives (words of substance) and adjectives (attributes of substances). It wasn't until the eighteenth century that grammarians began to recognize the distinctive properties of English, and gave separate word-class status to articles and adjectives. Dr Johnson, in the outline of English grammar included in his *Dictionary* (1755), doesn't give a complete listing of word classes, but he does distinguish articles and adjectives. This influenced the first school grammars, by Bishop Robert Lowth in 1762 and, following closely in his footsteps, the hugely influential grammar of Lindley Murray in 1795, used in schools for much of the nineteenth century.

These grammars recognized nine word classes – article, substantive, pronoun, adjective, verb, adverb, preposition, conjunction, interjection – and their approach has governed the way people think about parts of speech ever since. The only points of difference with modern approaches are that many grammars didn't mention the article as a separate part of speech, thinking that it wasn't worth setting up a separate class for just two words, *a* and *the*. And most modern grammars replaced *substantive* by *noun*. The longer word had come into grammatical use during the Middle Ages, as we saw with Jonson, to refer to 'a word denoting substance' – that is, a noun, as opposed to an adjective, which expressed only an attribute. The use of *substantive noun* was later shortened to *substantive*, which some grammars still use, but on the whole grammarians have preferred the shorter form, *noun*.

Modern grammars have actually resurrected the article as a word class, but in a different guise, as part of a new class usually called *determiner*. As the name suggests, this is a group of words whose function is to 'determine' the way we think of a noun. The following examples illustrate some of the most frequent determiners in English:

- *a cat* – this is the least specific way of talking about an individual noun; it could be any cat; the first English grammarians borrowed the term *article* from its use in Latin (*articulus*) and French, and called *a* the *indefinite article*.
- *the cat* – we have a particular instance of the noun in mind; it's now an identifiable or definable cat; so *the* came to be called the *definite article*.
- *this cat* – we are locating the noun as being near to us, in space, time or more abstractly; grammars took over the Latin term *demonstrativus* meaning 'serving to point out or indicate', and called it a *demonstrative* word, along with its plural *these*.
- *that cat* – we are locating the noun as being further away from us, in space, time, or more abstractly; another demonstrative, along with its plural *those*.
- *my, your, his* (etc.) *cat* – we are identifying the noun as belonging to someone; these words are usually described as *possessive*.

The determiner class isn't very large, but it conveniently brings together a set of words that otherwise are left to fend for themselves, such as *some, any, each, every, either* and *neither*. It's a good example of what happens when grammarians stop looking at a language through Latin spectacles and begin to describe it in its own terms. And it's a class that was extremely important to Suzie, especially when she realized what *my* meant.

Interlude: Learn by heart

The frontispiece to *The Play Grammar*, published in 1848 (see
also p. 88), with its companion verse entitled 'The Nine Parts
of Speech: a rhyme to be learned by heart'.

1. Three little words we often see
Are ARTICLES – *a, an,* and *the.*

2. A NOUN's the name of any *thing,*
As *house,* or *garden, hoop,* or *swing.*

3. ADJECTIVES tell the kind of Noun,
As *great, small, pretty, white,* or *brown.*

4. Instead of Nouns, the PRONOUNS stand;
Her head, *his* face, *your* arm, *my* hand.

5. VERBS tell of something being done;
To *read, write, count, sing, jump,* or *run.*

6. How things are done, the ADVERBS tell,
As *slowly, quickly, ill,* or *well.*

7. CONJUNCTIONS join the words together,
As men *and* women, wind *and* weather.

8. The PREPOSITIONS stand before
A Noun, – as *in,* or *through* the door.

9. The INTERJECTION shows surprise,
As *oh!* how pretty; *ah!* how wise.

The whole are called Nine Parts of Speech,
Which reading, writing, speaking teach.

What sentences do

While Suzie was sorting out the rules governing word forms, during her third year, she was also rapidly increasing her awareness of the different functions of sentences. Why do we use a sentence? The purposes include describing, enquiring, ordering, persuading, promising, warning ... a host of intentions that will take Suzie into adult life. But as early as fifteen months, as we saw in Chapter 1, she was manipulating her one-word sentences to express some of them.

I used to leave an audio recorder on for long periods, to capture what my kids were saying. (That's how linguists interested in child language acquisition used to get their information. When a colleague had a new baby, I used to send the parents a greetings card, with the message 'Congratulations on the birth of fresh data'.) And one day I heard the sequence I mentioned at the beginning of Chapter 1, which showed that Suzie knew that sentences don't all have the same purpose.

It was the time of day when I would come home from the university. She heard footsteps on the gravel path outside the kitchen and said *Dada?*, with a rising tone. When I came into the room, she pointed and said *Dada*, with a falling tone. And then, with both arms outstretched, she said *Dada*, with an insistent level tone. The first was clearly a question: 'Is that Daddy?' The second was just as clearly a statement: 'There's Daddy.' And the third was patently a command:

'Pick me up, Daddy.' She had some exclamations too, such as 'Bye-bye.'

At the two-word stage, she began to consolidate her aware-ness of these different sentence functions. Towards the end of her second year, she was saying more specific questions and commands, such as *Where Daddy?* and *Look me.* Then, as her sentences got longer, she noticed the crucial change that makes a statement different from a question in English: the order of the subject and verb is inverted.

That is Miffy > Is that Miffy?

It seems like a very simple rule, but it hides some complica-tions that it would take her some time to work out.

In particular, she had trouble (as does everyone learning English) with questions that begin with a question-word, such as *where, when,* and *what.* She made the logical assump-tion that, because words like *where* already ask a question, it isn't necessary to invert the order of subject and verb as well – which would be like asking the question all over again. So she said such things as:

Where Daddy is going? *instead of* Where is Daddy going?
Where you have put it? *instead of* Where have you put it?

Eventually, she got them right. It's another important lesson: grammar doesn't work in logical ways.

A child's sentence functions blossom in the third year – as parents very well know when they're at the receiving end of an interminable series of *why* questions. Commands develop too, with variants such as 'You sit there' and 'Let's go in the garden.' So do exclamations, with fuller sentences such as 'What a mess!' supplementing exclamatory noises such as 'Wow', 'Oh', and 'Yuk'. All four sentence functions were well established in Suzie by age three.

Keyword: functions

Grammarians had little trouble finding ways to describe the main meanings conveyed by sentences – what are usually called sentence *functions*. There are everyday words that capture the chief intentions being conveyed, and I used them above: *statement, question, command, exclamation*. English grammars do sometimes use alternatives – such as *interrogative* rather than *question*, or *directive* or *imperative* instead of *command* – so be prepared for some variation as you dip into a grammar.

The reason there are alternative terms is that no one word can capture all the functions that each type of sentence conveys.

- Statements do more than describe a state of affairs, e.g. they can be used to warn ('Entry is prohibited'), promise ('I'll make a donation'), or express an action ('I resign').
- Questions do more than ask for information, e.g. they can be used to threaten ('Are you looking at me?'), obtain agreement ('They're late again, aren't they?'), or make an emphatic point ('Who would have thought it?').
- Commands do more than give an order, e.g. they can be used to suggest ('Let's stay a few more minutes'), direct ('Turn left at the church'), or warn ('Mind the gap between the train and the platform').
- Exclamations do more than express a sudden emotion, e.g. they can be used as an affirmation of solidarity ('Cheers!'), or a congratulation or commiseration ('Happy Birthday!').

Regardless of the terminology used, grammars always

began with the description of statements. The reason for this priority stems, once again, from the philosophical way in which the classical writers approached the study of language, concerned to analyse how sentences described reality. Their interest was in the truth or falsity of statements, and that focus gave the statement function a privileged status which continued when grammars came to be written. Ever since, students have begun their study of a language by learning how it forms statements, and moving on to questions, commands, and exclamations later. Statements are seen as the basic form.

As far as the first English grammars were concerned, a sentence had to express one of these four functions. Modern approaches take a broader approach, recognizing that there are sentences that don't fit comfortably into any of these types. A good example is the *echo* sentence – the sort of thing we say when we want to query or challenge what someone else has just said.

A. I'm going to drive. B. You're going to drive?
A. Have you read the paper? B. Have I read the paper?
A. Go by train. B. Go by train?
A. Congratulations! B. Congratulations?

The reason for the echo is various. The second speaker might be surprised, critical, angry, dismissive ... But it's evident that this communicative strategy applies to all four kinds of sentence, and thus needs to be described separately.

Older grammars ignored the echo sentence, because they were based almost entirely on a description of written language, where such sequences are unusual, apart from in novels. They are a feature of the dynamic interaction that is typical of everyday conversation – a genre that grammarians failed to describe until the linguistic approaches of the mid-twentieth century.

As soon as the spoken language is taken into account, all sorts of sentences are encountered that can't be described as statements, questions, commands, or exclamations. How, for example, do we handle utterances such as *yes* and *no*? *Hello* and *goodbye*? *Thanks* and *sorry*? *Good morning* and *good night*? *OK*?

These sentences defy description using traditional terms, and modern grammars vary in the way they handle them. Some force them into the category of exclamations. Some attempt a classification of their function in a discourse, using such labels as responses, greetings, farewells, calls and apologies. Some view them as shortened forms of 'proper' sentences: *thanks*, for example, would be short for 'I give you thanks', *hello* short for 'I say hello'. Some simply group them as a category of 'sentences that have no structure', calling them by such names as *minor* or *irregular*. I like *minor sentences*, personally, as it allows me a nice contrast with the fully structured sentences in English, which I call *major sentences*.

Because minor sentences lack the complexities of the major grammatical structures of a language, learners pick them up quickly. People who speak no French usually know such words as *oui* and *merci*. And Suzie had acquired a fair number of English minor sentences by age three. Indeed, at around this age parents begin to draw attention to some of them as part of a focus on being polite: *please, thank you* (or simply *ta*), *sorry, pardon* ... Most of us recall parental injunctions such as 'Don't say what, say pardon!' or (in response to a request) 'I haven't heard that little word yet.' Little words they may be; but without them, conversations would be impossible.

Interlude: The first modern English grammarian

The remarkable John Wallis (1616–1703) was the first to call for a new, non-Latin approach to English grammar. A professor at Oxford, who helped to found the Royal Society in 1660, he wrote on mathematics, cryptography, logic, theology and music, as well as language. In his *Grammatica Linguae Anglicanae* ('Grammar of the English Language'), written in Latin, he makes it very clear that his intention is to break away from the Latin grammatical tradition. He writes that his procedure is 'a completely new method, which has its basis not, as is customary, in the structure of the Latin language but in the characteristic structure of our own' (p. xxvi). He keeps Latin terminology in his description, he says, chiefly because the terms are so well known, but his approach is unequivocal:

> English, in common with nearly all modern languages, differs enormously in syntax from Greek and Latin (the main reason being that in English we do not distinguish different cases). Few people recognise this when describing our language and other modern languages, and, consequently, the task is usually made more complicated than it need be. (p. 76, *Grammar of the English Language*, ed. J. A. Kemp, 1972)

This could have been written by any twentieth-century linguist. But for over 300 years his linguistic insight was ignored.

8

Sentence building

As Suzie's sentence functions developed, in her third year, so too did her ability to build up the different patterns that make up the major sentences in English. She'd already learned the basic principle – that a sentence has two main parts – and between eighteen months and two had produced hundreds of two-part sentences, as we saw in Chapter 2. She'd also learned that the order of these parts expresses different kinds of meaning: *daddy push* is different from *push daddy*. In the first, *daddy* is the doer of the action; in the second, he is the receiver of the action.

She'd also learned that, even if the order stayed the same, the two parts might relate to each other in different ways: *drink milk* isn't the same as *drink there*. The first expresses an action and the entity it affects; the second expresses an action and where it takes place. Sentences of this kind display an emerging awareness of another important grammatical principle in English: words can play different roles in a sentence.

The obvious next step was to combine these different roles. Suzie wanted to say more ambitious things, such as *me push daddy* contrasting with *daddy push me* – that somebody does something to someone. She wanted to locate the actions that people do, and say things like *mummy go car* and *dolly sleep bed* – that somebody does something somewhere. She wanted to describe people or objects in sentences, and say things like *my dress is pretty* or *mummy is asleep* – that someone or something has an attribute. With the mobile curiosity that two-year-olds have, she wanted to make all sorts of new observations and interrogate the world around her in increasingly inquisitive ways – which meant working out the sentence patterns that would allow her to say them.

It's another big step: the sentences now have three main parts, each of which could be just one word, as in the above examples, or could be phrases, so that the sentences might have four or more words:

dolly	sleep	pram
dolly	sleep	in pram
my dolly	sleep	pram
my dolly	do sleep	in pram

She was certainly up to the task of saying sentences of this length. As we saw in Chapter 4, with *little girl is eating*, she was already producing sentences of three or four words, using phrases that enabled her to describe small pictures (Chapter 3) in greater detail. Now she was in a position to use this length to extend her big-picture skills (Chapter 2) to talk about the world in more adventurous ways. This is where things start to become more difficult, as there are quite a few options to take on board. But within a year she had learned them all.

By age three, she was using sentences displaying remarkable syntactic progress, such as:

I put the ice cream on the table very carefully, Mummy.

This has five main parts, each of which expresses a different meaning:

I	the doer of the action
put	the action

the ice cream	the entity directly affected by the action
on the table	the place of the action
very carefully	the manner of the action

To keep up with Suzie, we have to find a way of describing each of these parts and meanings, and – if the description of English is to be comprehensive – work out just how many other options the language provides.

Keywords: elements and roles

To avoid a confusion with the rather vague *parts* (as in 'parts of speech'), modern grammarians use other terms to describe the main bits of a sentence, such as *unit, constituent,* or *element.* Similarly, to avoid the very general associations of the word *meaning,* they describe the jobs these elements perform in a sentence as *semantic roles* or *thematic roles.* I shall use *element* and *semantic role* in what follows.

It wasn't until the emergence of modern linguistics that a clear description of all the possibilities in English sentences came to be made, and the result was surprising. It turned out that there were only five elements to take into account, and these were combined in a remarkably small number of ways. Labelling the elements was fairly straightforward; defining their semantic roles proved to be more of a problem.

One of the commonest combinations expresses the notion that 'someone does something that affects some person or thing'. Grammarians kept the old terms of *subject* (S) and *verb* (V) for the first two elements, and (during the eighteenth century) added *object* (O) for the third. So a sentence such as the following would be analysed like this:

Chris kicked the ball
  S   V   O

They appreciated the need to explain what these terms meant. Bishop Lowth, for example, describes the subject as the Agent, 'the thing chiefly spoken of' – a perspective that has become a major feature of present-day approaches.

One of the insights of linguistics was to demonstrate that the situation is more complicated than the early grammars suggested. For example, it would hardly be right to call all subjects 'agents' or 'actors', in view of sentences like these:

<u>Suzie</u> felt happy.
<u>Chris</u> has a cold.

We need a different label to capture what is going on here. Because Suzie and Chris are experiencing the happiness and the cold, some grammarians call them *experiencers*. You'll encounter several new terms like this in modern approaches, as analysts identify all the roles that sentence elements convey.

Verbs proved to be just as multifaceted. For centuries, grammarians had described verbs as 'doing words', and that's the way they're still often characterized in school. But many verbs seem not to be 'doing' anything at all. Take the two I've just used: *proved* and *seem*. It would be more accurate to say they express 'appearance' rather than 'action'. To handle cases like this, modern grammars usually distinguish *stative* (related to *static*) or *state* verbs as opposed to *dynamic* or *action* verbs. And they classify the different kinds of meaning that stative verbs express, such as possession (*Chris has a car*), feelings (*Chris loves oranges*), perceptions (*Chris heard a noise*), mental processes (*Chris knows a lot*), and general notions of existence and identity (*Chris is a doctor*). None of these are 'actions' like *kick*, *eat*, and *go*.

It isn't just that the meaning of stative verbs is different from that of dynamic verbs. English grammar actually treats them differently. Dynamic verbs have alternative 'progressive' (or 'continuous') forms such as:

> Chris kicks the ball. – Chris is kicking the ball.
> Chris paints pictures. – Chris is painting pictures.

Stative verbs typically don't do this. We don't say:

> Chris is having a car.
> Chris is seeming fine.

But there are some interesting exceptions, as my next Interlude shows.

The element following the verb was also seen to vary depending on the kind of verb used in the sentence. These two sentences show the difference:

> Chris called a doctor.
> Chris became a doctor.

In the first sentence, there's no identity between the subject and what follows the verb: *the doctor* and *Chris* are two different people. In the second sentence, there is identity: *Chris* = *doctor*. So if we call *a doctor* in the first sentence an *object*, we need a different term for it in the second. Grammarians in the nineteenth century came up with a solution: *complement* (C) – from Latin *complementum* – an element that 'completes' the meaning of some other element in a sentence. All the following sentences have complements:

Chris	became	a doctor.
Chris	is	a doctor.
Chris	is	excited.
S	V	C

As with the contrast between stative and dynamic verbs,

sentences with an object work in a grammatically different way from those with a complement. For example, we can say the first of the following sentences, but not the second:

Chris saw two doctors.   *but not* Chris became two doctors.
Chris was seen by a doctor. *but not* Chris was become by a doctor.

The notions of subject, object, and complement handled the way verbs affected 'somethings' and 'someones'; but that left the 'somewheres' and 'somewhens' and 'somehows', used in sentences like these:

Chris kicked the ball there.
Chris kicked the ball yesterday.
Chris kicked the ball forcefully.

The Latin grammarians saw these additional elements as adding something to the meaning of the verb: where did the kicking take place? When did it take place? How did it take place? So they called them *adverbs* – literally, 'to' (in the sense of 'reaching back to') the verb – and that is how English grammarians used the term, from the earliest days. So the analyses looked like this:

Chris   kicked   the ball   forcefully.
S   V   O   A

The study of adverbs turned out to be more complicated than people expected. For a start, this word class has more semantic roles than the expression of the time, place, and manner of an action. Adverbs can convey frequency (*Chris kicked the ball often*), degree (*Chris hardly kicked the ball*), uncertainty (*Chris probably kicked the ball*), and much more. And some adverbs seem to apply to whole sentences rather than just the verbs (*Fortunately, Chris kicked the ball*).

Adverbs are also more mobile in a sentence. There aren't many places in a sentence where a subject, a verb, an object, and a complement can go; but adverbs seem able to go almost anywhere:

> Forcefully, Chris kicked the ball.
> Chris forcefully kicked the ball.
> Chris kicked, forcefully, the ball.

The options aren't all equally likely, and there are differences of emphasis and style, but no other element of a sentence is as versatile as the adverb.

Another unique feature of adverbs is that there's no limit to the number you can have in a sentence. Sentences such as the above have just one subject, one verb, one object, and one complement; but we can add as many adverbs as we like:

> Chris probably kicked the ball there yesterday forcefully
> ...

There are complications, of course. As soon as we string adverbs together, we find that some orders are more acceptable than others. We're less likely to hear someone say:

> Chris kicked the ball forcefully yesterday there.

Working out why some word orders are possible, some are uncertain, and some are impossible is one of the intriguing challenges facing researchers in English grammar.

And one other thing about adverbs. Just as nouns can expand into noun phrases and verbs into verb phrases, so adverbs can expand into adverb phrases, such as these:

Chris kicked the ball <u>in the garden</u>.
Chris kicked the ball <u>yesterday morning</u>.
Chris kicked the ball <u>with great force</u>.

Now we need a term so that we can talk about adverbs and adverb phrases at the same time, as well as anything else that can function in the way an adverb does. Some linguists adopted *adverbial* – actually a medieval alternative for *adverb*, but now used with this broader meaning. Others opted for another old term, used since the sixteenth century (and employed in Chapter 2): *adjunct*.

So, where is Suzie up to? At age three she has learned to say, with just occasional errors, all the main sentence patterns. She knows most of the roles that sentence elements convey. She knows all the sentence functions. We might be forgiven for thinking that she has now mastered English grammar, but we would be wrong, for she is about to face the biggest grammatical challenge of all.

Interlude: Grammatically precocious

Lord Macauley

Presumably the young Thomas Babington Macaulay would have taken grammatical terminology (and jigsaws?) in his stride. Most of the stories circulating about him in the nineteenth century are probably apocryphal, but it is said that he didn't speak until he was four, and then came out with fully formed sentences. Apparently his first sentence emerged when he was visiting a neighbour's house with his parents, and a hot drink was accidentally spilt on his legs. Asked by his hostess whether he was hurt, he supposedly replied: 'Madam, the agony is somewhat abated.' Later, asked why he hadn't spoken earlier, he observed: 'Hitherto, nothing of sufficient significance has warranted my verbal attention.'

9

Story time

Until she was about three, every sentence Suzie uttered consisted of a single subject+predicate selection made from the sentence elements subject, verb, object, complement, or adverbial. She used them in all her sentence functions, and was able to produce utterances consisting of ten words or more. After hearing a fairy story, she said, spontaneously, 'The little girl did see the prince in his beautiful palace.' But that was it. Subject + verb + object + adverbial. It was a single observation, not a retelling of the story.

Then, as she approached the end of her third year, she learned a word that must initially have seemed quite magical to her: *and*. It's a word that opens up unlimited possibilities. When you've learned *and*, you realize that you can keep a sentence going for ever and … ever and … ever and …

She tried it out first, as most children do, by building up short little-picture phrases. A car was no longer just clean, it was *nice and clean*. *Mummy and Daddy* went in a train. She certainly appreciated the power of *and* when she had to decide what toy to take in the car with her:

I want teddy and my dolly and my monkey and my elephant and …

Mum had to break in to stop the flow. It was quite a small car.

Then she made the leap: she started to use *and* to link

whole sentences – first, toe-in-the-water sequences, placing little demand on her memory, such as:

> Mummy pushed the pram and Daddy pushed the pram

then much more ambitious sequences – such as this one about a cat:

> Katie seed a big bird in the garden and – she runned after it and – and – and the bird went up in a tree and – she climbed – she – she climbed up and it went away …

That's a transcription of what she actually said, hesitations and all, when she was three and a quarter. And it shows an interesting feature: what speech pathologists call 'normal non-fluency'. It might seem at first as if she was stammering, but she isn't. When children (or adults) stammer, there are clear signs of their frustration, as they try to get their sounds out. There's no sign of that here. Suzie was obviously having difficulty keeping all the parts of her long story in mind, but she wasn't at all bothered by it. All her listener had to do was to be patient: she would get there in the end.

Why was she having difficulty? Because of all the mental processing she was having to do as she told her story. Storytelling is a multi-directional thing: you have to focus on what you're currently saying while remembering what you've already said and anticipating what you're about to say. Suzie is used to expressing her thoughts as single 'chunks' of subject+predicate information. Now she needs to string them together so that they make sense as a story. It's hard, at first. Quite a strain on her young memory. So she pauses, at the end of each chunk, while she works out how to say the next one. But her instinct is to keep the story going (children are natural storytellers), so she lets her listener know that there's more to come by getting the word *and* in quickly, and then pausing while she thinks – and if she needs still more time, she repeats it.

The non-fluency lasted a couple of months in her case. With some children, it can last as long as six months. With others, there's little or no non-fluency at all. But at the end of this period, fluent storytelling is in place. Children are now using their grammar to create not just sentences, but discourses.

Keyword: clause

For the grammarian, stringing sentences together presents a new kind of problem. If *Mummy went in a train* is a sentence, and *Daddy went in a train* is a sentence, then what do we do with *Mummy went in a train and Daddy went in a train*, which is also a sentence? It would sound confusing to say it is a sentence consisting of two sentences. To avoid the problem, early grammarians talked vaguely about sentence 'parts' or 'members' or 'segments'. But eventually, they came up with the term *clause*.

This term is first recorded in English in the thirteenth century, where it seems to mean (following *clausula* in Latin – literally, a 'little closing') a short sentence expressing a maxim, conclusion, or succinct thought of some kind. The various units of meaning in the Lord's Prayer, for example, were called clauses: 'Hallowed be thy name', 'Thy will be done'. By the time that Dr Johnson compiled his *Dictionary* (1755), usage had become more focused. He defines *clause* with increasing technical precision:

A sentence; a single part of a discourse; a subdivision of a larger sentence; so much of a sentence as is to be construed together.

Nineteenth-century grammars took the notion a stage further, and by the time of Henry Alford's *The Queen's English* in the 1860s were using the term routinely for a subject+predicate unit that can either stand on its own (it is an *independent* clause) or become a part of a larger sentence. So Suzie's sentence would be analysed like this:

SENTENCE

Mummy pushed the pram and Daddy pushed the pram.
CLAUSE   CLAUSE

The connecting word was seen to be a *conjunction* – long recognized as a separate word class (see Chapter 6).

Then the terms for these larger constructions began to proliferate. As with many other areas of knowledge during that century, there was a mania for classifying and cataloguing everything, and grammar wasn't exempt. Writers needed names for these smaller and larger sentences. This is where readers new to grammatical analysis need to take a deep breath.

It took a while to achieve consensus. Most grammarians opted instinctively for *simple sentence* as the obvious term to describe a sentence consisting of just one clause. But there was some uncertainty over the best term to describe sentences with more than one clause: some liked *complex sentence*, some liked *compound sentence*. In the end, both were used, but in different ways. Grammarians drew attention to the fact that the conjunctions were of different kinds. Some, such as *and*, connected clauses that were of the same type. In the above example, each clause could stand on its own as a separate sentence. The term *coordinate*, in its everyday sense of 'equal in status', 'of the same rank', was used for such conjunctions as *and, but, either,* and *or*, which all seemed to work in the same way, connecting independent clauses.

Coordinating conjunctions became the most widely used term, though some grammarians, finding this a bit of a mouthful, later opted for *coordinators*. A clause that followed a coordinator was called a *coordinate clause*. And sentences containing clauses linked by coordinators were called *compound sentences*.

Other conjunctions, such as *after*, worked differently:

SENTENCE
Mummy pushed the pram after Daddy pushed the pram.
CLAUSE   CLAUSE

Here the two clauses are not of the same type. The first clause is independent: it can stand on its own as a separate sentence. The second clause can't stand on its own. *After Daddy pushed the pram* depends on the other clause in order to make sense. Some writers therefore called a clause like this a *dependent clause*, but the term that eventually achieved more widespread use was *subordinate clause*. Conjunctions such as *because, when,* and *after* were consequently called *subordinating conjunctions* – with *subordinators* a more succinct alternative. And sentences containing clauses linked by subordinators were called *complex sentences*. It was never a very satisfactory solution, as the word *complex* has such a general meaning. Any lengthy sentence might be called complex, regardless of the kinds of clause it contains. But the term has lasted, and is still used in some modern grammars.

As always happens in grammar, one problem solved leads to another problem identified. If a sentence contains a subordinate clause, what should we call the other clause – the one on which it depends, and which can stand alone? The term *main clause* came into use in the mid-nineteenth century, and soon became the industry standard.

The search for comprehensiveness was on. Grammars had to describe all possibilities. So, what should we call sentences that contain *both* a coordinate clause and a subordinate clause?

SENTENCE

Mummy pushed the pram and Daddy pushed the pram
when it was raining.
COORD. CLAUSE   SUBORD. CLAUSE

The answer was simple: if the first type produces a compound sentence and the second type produces a complex sentence, then a type that contains both should be called a *compound-complex sentence*. It was a solution that appealed to many, and it has stayed in use, though some modern grammarians – once again, finding it a bit of a mouthful – have opted for a more succinct label, such as *multiple sentence*.

The addition of *clause* to the repertoire of terms was a huge step forward for anyone writing within the European tradition of grammar study, and it continues to play a central part in many modern descriptions of English. But not all. When in the 1950s Noam Chomsky introduced his new approach to grammar, he didn't use the term *clause*. In English grammars based on his approach, you will see such terms as *conjoined sentence* for cases like coordination and *embedded sentence* for cases where one sentence is included within another.

The notion of clause also helped grammarians to describe another important feature of English syntax that hitherto had been presented obscurely or not at all. They realized that a subordinate clause depended on its main clause in very specific ways. Some subordinate clauses acted like adverbials:

Daddy pushed the pram <u>today</u>.   – the adverbial is
                                             an adverb
Daddy pushed the pram <u>this morning</u>. – the adverbial
                                             is an adverb
                                             phrase

So, to continue the reasoning ...

Daddy pushed the pram <u>when it was raining</u>.

Because the clause is doing the same job as an adverb, grammarians in this approach therefore called it an *adverb clause* (or *adverbial clause*).

Other subordinate clauses acted like subjects, objects, or complements. And because they were doing the same job as a noun, they were called *noun clauses* (or, using an adjective that became popular during the nineteenth century, *nominal clauses*). That handled cases like this:

<u>Chris</u> made sense. – the subject is a noun
<u>Her comments</u> made sense. – the subject is a noun phrase
<u>What she said</u> made sense. – the subject is a noun clause

and this:

Chris ate <u>sandwiches</u>. – the object is a noun
Chris ate <u>my sandwiches</u>. – the object is a noun phrase
Chris ate <u>what I had bought</u>. – the object is a noun clause

It's important to note that conjunctions in subordinate clauses are very different from those in coordinate clauses. Subordinate conjunctions like *when* and *what* have to be analysed as *part* of the clauses they introduce, because they are an essential part of the meaning these clauses convey. Coordinating conjunctions like *and* and *but* don't form part of the clauses they join. We could omit them without the meaning of the independent clauses being affected:

Mummy pushed the pram and Daddy pushed the pram.
Mummy pushed the pram; Daddy pushed the pram.

If we leave out the subordinating conjunction, we completely lose the meaning of what we're trying to say.

> Mummy pushed the pram after Daddy pushed the pram.
> Mummy pushed the pram; Daddy pushed the pram.

Getting to grips with the way clauses can be used within sentences is one of the trickiest aspects of grammatical analysis, because we're constantly having to think of the way the individual clauses operate as well as bear in mind the structure of the sentence as a whole. Children who suffer from some kind of language disability find real difficulty in mastering this stage of grammatical development. Some never manage it, so that they are never able to form coherent discourses. Adults with a language problem (such as those who lose their speech after a stroke) also often have the same difficulty. They can handle simple sentences, but their former narrative abilities have disappeared.

By contrast, Suzie's narrative skills went from strength to strength. By four, she was telling stories of considerable complexity, such as this extract from a retelling of 'The Three Little Pigs':

> One day they went out to build their houses. One built it of straw, one built it of sticks, and one built it of bricks. And the little busy brother knowed that in the woods there lived a big bad wolf, he need nothing else but to catch little pigs
> …

Imagine you are a teacher, and you had to correct the grammar of this story. You would mark *knowed* and *need* as errors. But otherwise – and allowing for the immature style – you would conclude, as at the end of Chapter 8, that Suzie has now indeed completed the learning of English grammar. And once again you would be wrong.

10
Connecting

People often say that children have completed the learning of the grammar of their language by the time they go to school, around the age of five. And on the surface, it would seem to be the case. Suzie still had occasional problems with irregular forms at age four, as illustrated by the sentences at the end of Chapter 9; but a year later these had disappeared. So now she was coming out with sentences like this:

> I'm not scared of ghosts and monsters like Scooby Doo is, cos they're on the telly, and he's got lots of friends to help him.

No errors here. Grammar game over, it would seem.

But if we start to look more carefully at how Suzie is talking, it becomes clear that the game isn't over. There's still some grammar left to learn. She doesn't make mistakes in what she actually says; but there are quite a few aspects of grammar that she hasn't tried to use at all. We can see this if we compare her sentences to those an adult would use when telling a story. In particular, adults link their sentences using a much wider range of connecting words than *and* and *cos*, such as *however, moreover, unfortunately, nevertheless*, and *as a matter of fact*. Suzie used none of these at age five.

She started trying some of them out soon after. From the stories she heard at bedtime, she picked up *fortunately* and *unfortunately*. When six-year-olds come out with such words, it's always a bit of a surprise, as their speech suddenly sounds very mature. I remember, when I was doing research into child language, and observing a class of six-year-olds, one of them put up her hand. 'What is it, Jane?' asked the teacher. And Jane replied: 'Actually, I want to go to the toilet.' It was the *actually* that caught my attention. This is quite an abstract notion, with its suggestion of 'as a matter of interest' or 'contrary to what you might think'. Jane hasn't got the word quite right, in this context, but we can see the way she's moving towards its proper usage. Suzie did the same sort of thing, along with other connecting words such as *anyway*, *besides*, and *after that*.

This was a general characteristic of Suzie's grammar, in her pre-school year. She would come out with a sentence that, on the surface, sounded fine. But when you examined the situation carefully, you could tell she hadn't fully understood the way English grammar worked. Her usage was only approximately right. For example, it took her some time to work out the subtle ways in which *because* is used. Sometimes she got it right:

You shouldn't throw rocks, because that will break windows.

Sometimes she got it wrong:

It's raining because the flowers are growing.

With examples like these, it's clear that her production – her ability to produce a grammatically correct sentence – is running ahead of her comprehension. We understand what she's getting at, but her grasp of 'cause and effect' still needs some attention. That's one of the things her schoolteachers will focus on, as she learns to read and write: comprehension.

Keyword: connectives

Sentences may be the building blocks of communication, but they are a means to an end, not an end in themselves. We do not usually speak and write in isolated sentences: we speak and write in the sentence-sequences I've been calling *discourses*. In speech, discourses include conversations, dialogues, monologues, lectures, sermons, and broadcasts; in writing, books, scripts, pamphlets, blogs, advertisements, and newspaper articles. We need grammar not only to make our sentences work successfully, but to make discourses work successfully too. Just as there are rules governing how we put words together to form an acceptable sentence, so there are rules governing how we put sentences together to form an acceptable discourse.

Early grammars largely ignored this wider perspective. Their focus was on the way sentences were formed. It wasn't until the linguistic approaches of the twentieth century that grammarians began to look at what happens to sentences when they are used in sequence. They found that there are quite a small set of features whose function is to link sentences in meaningful ways, and they described these as features of – the choice of term varied with the writer – sentence *connectivity, connection, coherence, cohesion, coordination*. In schools, when a new focus on grammar teaching evolved in the 1990s, the most widely used term to describe a feature with a sentence-connecting function was *connective*.

Six-year-old Jane's *actually*, and the other words and phrases shown above, form one type of connective – mainly adverbials of various kinds. In these next examples, the adverbial first expresses a time relationship, and then a relationship in which the speaker's attitude links the sentences.

Mary went to the cinema. <u>Afterwards</u>, she went to the restaurant.

Mary went to the cinema. <u>Unfortunately</u>, her friend couldn't go with her.

There are hundreds of ways in which *afterwards* could be replaced to express different kinds of time relationship: *later, next, after a while, eventually, subsequently* … A useful learning technique, often used in schools, is to practise making substitutions of this kind while being aware of the changes of meaning involved.

Pronouns are another way to show sentence connection. A written sentence such as *It was climbing up a tree* assumes that you know what the *it* refers to. The identity needs to be explained in another sentence – about a squirrel, for instance. Similarly, if we see *Mary found the box in the corner*, the use of *the* assumes that we know which box we're talking about. And a sentence like *John was quickest at finishing the puzzle* doesn't make much sense until we know with whom John is being compared.

Sometimes more than one word with a connective function occurs in a sentence. What would you make of someone saying *But she did so too*? This actually refers back to previous sentences in four different ways: the *but* expresses a contrast with something previously said; the *she* refers back to someone already mentioned; the *did so* refers to an action already mentioned; and the *too* suggests that someone else has done the same action. We need the context to make sense of it all. And we need to know the rules that English allows, as well as those that aren't, in order to make the sequence work. For instance, we can't say *We didn't so too*.

It takes children several years to master all these connectives in speech. Then, when they get to school, they have to learn to use them all over again in writing, in quite a short time, and that's when problems can arise. When she was about seven, Suzie wrote a story which began like this:

> Once upon a time there was a king who lived in a castle with his son. He was very handsome ...

From the writer's point of view, there was no problem: Suzie knew who was handsome. But from the reader's point of view, there was ambiguity. So the teacher marking her story red-circled the *he*, and wrote a question in the margin: 'who?' I remember having to explain why to Suzie, who couldn't see anything wrong with it. 'If you didn't know who was handsome, you could just have asked me,' she said. We spent quite a while talking about why this wasn't really possible in a book.

Later in her story, Suzie wrote this:

> ... he went into the forest and you know what there was a little house ...

That got another red mark: *you know what* was crossed through. That led to another discussion – this time about the differences between speech and writing.

This was one of the big lessons Suzie had to learn as soon as she went to school: that the grammar she had learned for listening and speaking wouldn't always work when it came to reading and writing. All her friends were in the same boat. More than at any time previously, when children arrive in school, they are brought face to face with the challenge of *style*.

Interlude: Did the teddy bear chase the elephant?

Typical puppets for use in a passive comprehension game

Here's an experiment anyone can do with a tame six-year-old, to show that grammatical production is sometimes ahead of comprehension.

Suzie came in crying one day, around age six, saying *I was stung by a big wasp*. I was so impressed by the grammar that I almost forgot the antihistamine. I would have expected her to say *A big wasp stung me*. That was the kind of sentence she had been using for years. I hadn't heard her use the other type before.

She was showing the grammatical distinction between a *passive* and an *active* sentence. In a passive sentence, the subject (*I*, in this example) is, literally, passive – waiting for the action to take place. In an active sentence, the subject (*A big wasp*) is doing the action. Both sentences mean the same thing, but the way they tell the story differs.

Passive sentences are useful in English because they allow people to say that something happened without having to say who did it. Science writers use them a lot, because a passive lets them say 'The mixture was poured into the beaker' instead of the uncomfortably personal 'I/we poured the mixture into the beaker.' But everyone uses passives some-times, saying such things as 'I've just had my house painted' or 'Two people have been killed in an accident' or 'Entry is prohibited.' People who recommend that the passive should be avoided – George Orwell was a famous instance – forget cases like this, where we want to report an action without naming the actor. Who has painted, killed, or prohibited? Often we don't know, or don't want to say. I'll go into the contrast in more detail in Chapter 16.

When do children come to learn that the change in the form of the verb between active and passive actually reverses the action? Not at six. I took a teddy and a elephant, and asked Suzie to show me 'The teddy is chasing the elephant.' She carried out the actions. Then I asked: 'Show me the teddy is chased by the elephant.' She made the teddy chase the ele-phant again! Most children would do the same at this age. A year later, she had grasped the difference, and made the elephant chase the teddy.

Why was she not able to do that when she could say *I was stung by a big wasp*? Probably because teddies and elephants can chase each other, whereas wasps and people don't sting each other. The wasp situation was a much easier state of affairs to understand and talk about, and putting *big wasp* at the end of the sentence, which the passive allowed her to do, gave it real emphasis. The experimental situation must have been more confusing. So, even though at six she appeared to have mastered the grammar of the passive sentence, it was evidently only a partial mastery at that age.

11

Talking about grammar

When children get to school, they do two linguistic things:
they learn more language – vocabulary especially – and they
learn to talk about language. Both are important. As with
any skill, it helps if you can talk about it and discuss it with
others.

In actual fact, before they get to school, children have
already encountered quite a few words for talking about language. It's a regular topic of conversation with parents and
caretakers. The words may not seem very technical, but they
are nonetheless building up a language-related vocabulary.
Here are some of the remarks I've heard parents say to their
pre-school children:

> I can't <u>understand</u> you.
> That's a clever thing to <u>say</u>.
> That <u>sounds</u> silly.
> Don't <u>shout</u>.
> What's that <u>called</u>?
> I'm going to <u>tell</u> you a <u>story</u>.
> I'll <u>write</u> your <u>name</u> on it.
> The wolf had a <u>big gruff voice</u>.
> Turn the <u>page</u>.

Some parents go much further, and teach their children all
the letters of the alphabet, before they go to school. Or some
of them:

That's a big O.
Lots of Xs. [i.e. kisses]
That's M for Mateo.

I've rarely heard grammar terms used, though, other than *word* (as in *naughty word*); or *sentence*, occasionally.

Things were different in the nineteenth century, if the children's books published in the Victorian era are to be believed. Then, grammatical terms were bandied about the tea table in the houses of well-to-do families. Children might play a game of grammatical 'consequences', which went like this:

Choose twelve nouns, and write one on each of a dozen cards.
Choose twelve verbs, and do the same.
Choose twelve adverbs, and do the same.
Then, on twelve cards, write imaginative variants of 'The consequence was …'
Shuffle each group of cards and place each group in a labelled container.
Four players each take a container, randomly pick a card, and read out what it says, starting with the noun, then the verb, then the adverb, then the consequence.

The fun lay in the unexpected nature of the generated sequences. An example given in *The Play Grammar* (see p. 49) went like this:

John: The little dog –
Mary: waddled –
Lucy: methodically –
George: The consequence was he was promoted.

A century later, we find the same sort of grammatical exercise in Maureen Vidler's *Find a Story* series, with the structural choices there presented horizontally across cut pages. You read downwards, choosing one item from each line. The series starts with simple sentences and builds up to more complex alternatives, with rather more daring text, such as:

> Did you know / who told you / would you have guessed
> / ...
> that huge hairless / that almost all fat / that millions of
> / ...
> poodles / teachers / policemen / ...
> look much better / never tire of / are keen on / ...
> eating cabbage leaves? /standing on their heads? /
> wallowing in mud? / ...

You can tell 150,000 stories this way, says the book blurb.

Many other variants have been devised, both at home and in school, with the aim of making children aware of the way sentences are structured. They often incorporated grammatical terms. Another Victorian pastime was called 'Conundrums'.

> What conjunction holds liquids? [But – t]
> When is a door an adverb? [When it's a-jar]
> What verb is good to carry water in? [Can]
> Out of which pronoun are coals brought? [Mine]
> What adverb wears a shoe? [A-foot]

You may have seen some of these before. They used to turn up in books like *1000 Jokes for Kids*, or pop out of a Christmas cracker. Maybe they still do.

Keyword: metalanguage

The term *metalanguage* arrived in English in the 1930s, used chiefly by logicians and linguists to refer to 'the language we use to talk about language'. It was a convenient way of referring to all linguistic terminology at once, and its convenience has given it a more widespread use outside of linguistics. In particular, in relation to the teaching of language in schools, the phrase *metalinguistic awareness* became widely used during the 1990s – in the UK, as a result of its use in influential government reports on English teaching.

The basic idea was that children who are lagging behind in their linguistic skills would make greater progress if they were able to step back and reflect on what it is they are doing when they listen, speak, read, or write. 'There is no reason,' said the hugely influential 1988 *Report of the Committee of Inquiry into the Teaching of English Language*, chaired by Sir John Kingman, 'why the subject of the English language should not be discussed like any other', and it went on:

> pupils need to have their attention drawn to what they
> are doing and why they are doing it because this is helpful
> to the development of their language ability ... Teaching
> language must involve talking about language ...

It took a long time to work out how exactly this was to be done, and thirty years later the issue continues to be debated – not least, in relation to grammar, with its multiplicity of terms. But the principle was generally accepted, and its relevance came to be repeatedly demonstrated in research studies. There seemed to be a strong correlation between children's progress in English and their ability to talk about the language.

Why this is so isn't entirely clear. Which is the direction of influence? Is it the case that those children who are making good progress in language learning are readier to pick up linguistic terms? Or is it the other way round: that children who are taught linguistic terms find them helpful in improving their abilities in oracy and literacy? Or is it some combination of these two factors?

An analogy. Do we need to know all the technical terms to do with a car in order to be a good driver? I know someone who is a brilliant auto-mechanic, but he's a terrible driver. Clearly, to be a good driver we need skills that go beyond technical awareness, such as patience, calmness, and sensitivity to other road users. On the other hand, it's likely that the more we *can* talk about our car, the more we'll appreciate its strengths and limitations, which is bound to have a positive influence on the way we drive. And in many countries, we won't be able to drive at all without passing a test that shows we have mastered the terms contained in a Highway Code.

Back to language. It's important to appreciate that, unlike car driving, the learning of metalinguistic terms is to some extent a natural process. If words such as *name* and *say* are a normal part of parent-child conversation, then we'd expect them to appear quite early in children's speech. And this is what we find when we go looking.

In the 1980s, Bridie Raban, a researcher at the University of Reading, carried out a survey of the spoken vocabulary of 96 five-year-old children, using recordings of their spontaneous speech at home. She collected over 21,000 utterances altogether, which represented just under 4,000 different words. The sample contained a number of language-related terms, mainly general words to do with speaking and early literacy: *answer, ask, book, call, letter, mean, name, page, question, read, say, shout, shush, sing, sound, story, talk, tell, understand, word, write.* The children said such things as 'What does it say?', 'Read me a story', and 'What does factory mean?' They were already on the metalinguistic road.

On the other hand, there's not much sign of anything grammatical in that list. The only items we might expect to find in a grammar book are *word, question,* and *answer*. This isn't because five-year-olds aren't capable of handling technical or abstract terms. Other words in Raban's list included *apparatus, chrysalid, emergency, microphone, nuisance, ordinary, parachute, programme, spacesuit,* and *vacuuming*. People regularly underestimate the size and complexity of children's vocabulary. But it does seem that grammatical metalanguage is not a feature of home conversations. As *The Play Grammar* illustrates, this wasn't always so.

Interlude: Victorian playfulness

An illustration from The Play Grammar

The Play Grammar has a subtitle: *The Elements of Grammar Explained in Easy Games.* It was written by a well-known educational children's writer, Julia Corner – 'Miss Corner', as she is named on the title page. The book came out in 1848. I have the 25th edition, 'enlarged and improved', published over twenty years later. It was clearly hugely popular. Here's the opening chapter.

'Oh! MAMMA,' said little Fanny, one morning, after breakfast, 'will you tell Herbert and me how to play the game you spoke of last night, and which you called the Play Grammar?'

'Do, mamma!' exclaimed Herbert. 'I should like to know more about it.'

'And so should I,' repeated Fanny; 'for my birth-day will soon be here, and our cousins are coming to spend the day, you know; so we could amuse them with it, and puzzle them, as you puzzled us last night. Julia is fond of puzzles and riddles.'

'Well, my dears,' said their mamma 'I have not the least objection; so, if you like, we will begin now.'

The Play Grammar was brought, and the two children sat down at the table with their mamma, who asked Fanny how many days would elapse before her birth-day.

The little girl counted the days with her fingers, and found there would be twelve.

'Then you will just have time to get through our Play Grammar,' said her mamma, 'for it is in ten divisions, and we will take one of them each day.'

'Will this game teach us grammar?' asked Herbert.

'Yes, my dear, it will teach you something of grammar; in the same way that your puzzle-maps teach you something of geography.'

'Oh! that will be capital,' said Herbert; 'because we shall learn, and be amused too. I am impatient to begin.'

And sure enough, over the next ten days, they work/play their way through each part of speech – nominative cases, neuter genders, pluperfect tenses, subjunctive moods, and all – and, according to Miss Corner, have a great time. Grammar, for these children, was definitely glamorous, despite mamma's resolutely Latinate approach.

12

Up with which we will not put

When children arrive in school, their spoken grammatical abilities are well advanced but their metalinguistic awareness of grammar is roughly – nil. That's the conclusion I draw from the examples of child development in Chapter 9 and the reports of parent and child usage in Chapter 11. It's a huge gap, and for the past 250 years, teachers and textbook writers have wondered how best to bridge it.

For the early grammarians and schoolteachers, there was no issue. All they felt they had to do was introduce children to the way English was presented in the available textbooks, which all used the prestigious Latin model. Parents too: that's what Fanny and Herbert's mamma is doing in *The Play Grammar*. In the late eighteenth century, people had an acknowledged introduction to follow – Robert Lowth's *Introduction to English Grammar* (1762) – and from the end of the century schools everywhere – in America as well as Britain – were using the Lowth-indebted *English Grammar* of Lindley Murray (1795).

The influence of these grammars can't be overstated. Lowth's book had 45 editions by 1800. Murray's eventually sold over twenty million copies, one of the bestselling books of the early nineteenth century. Even Murray's detractors acknowledged his supremacy. In 1839, the writer Thomas de Quincey, who was hugely critical of Murray's approach (it is 'full of atrocious blunders'), reflects gloomily on the way his grammar 'reigns despotically through the young ladies' schools, from the Orkneys to the Cornish Scillys'. Charles Dickens wasn't impressed either, judging by his description in *The Old Curiosity Shop* (Chapter 29) of Mrs Jarley's efforts to attract a new class of audience to her waxworks:

> these audiences were of a very superior description, including a great many young ladies' boarding-schools, whose favour Mrs Jarley had been at great pains to conciliate, by altering the face and costume of Mr Grimaldi as clown to represent Mr Lindley Murray as he appeared when engaged in the composition of his English Grammar
> …

Punch magazine in 1863 even contains a poem about Murray:

> There was a young lady of Surrey,
> Who always would talk in a hurry,
> Being called by her Pa,
> She replied 'here I are,'
> And he said, 'Go and read Lindley Murray.'

Surely there can be no greater accolade, than to be the punch-line of a limerick?

Murray's influence extended throughout the nineteenth century, and into the twentieth through many derivative works. But at the same time there was a growing unease that this was not the best way to be introducing children to English grammar. Only the occasional voice heeded John Wallis's warning (p. 57) that the Latinate approach made the study of grammar 'more complicated than it need be'. Essayist William Hazlitt was one. In 1829 he ferociously attacked that approach in an article called 'English grammar' in *The Atlas* periodical. Here are some choice bits:

This is one of those subjects on which the human understanding has played the fool ...

The Definitions alone are able to corrupt a whole generation of ingenuous youth. They seem calculated for no other purpose than to mystify and stultify the understanding ...

Thus to instance in the present noun – A case, Of a case, To a case, A case, O case, From a case – they tell you that the word *case* is here its own nominative, genitive, dative, accusative, vocative, and ablative, though the deuce of any case – that is, inflection of the noun – is there in the case. Nevertheless, many a pedagogue would swear till he was black in the face that it is so; and would lie awake many a restless night boiling with rage and vexation that any one should be so lost to shame and reason as to suspect that there is here also a distinction without a difference.

If a system were made in burlesque and purposely to call into question and expose its own nakedness, it could not go beyond this, which is gravely taught in all seminaries, and patiently learnt by all school-boys ...

... and schoolgirls. Poor Fanny and Herbert had to do exactly that, on their Ninth Day. Mamma introduces them to three of the cases:

Nouns or pronouns are in the nominative case when they come before a verb; they are in the objective case when they come after a verb, or preposition; and they are in the possessive case when they imply the possession of property.

She gives the children some examples:

When I say 'the sun shines;' *shines,* a verb, following the noun *sun,* places the *sun* in the *nominative* case.

Or, when I say, 'the clouds hide the sun;' the noun, *sun*, coming after the verb *hide*, places it in the *objective* case.

She gives the children a test pair of sentences showing the different cases: *your cousin writes* and *someone writes to your cousin*, and asks:

'Can either of you say what causes the difference?'
A rather long silence followed the question; and neither of the children seemed willing to venture a reply.

I'm not surprised. But mamma persists, and, of course, they get it right in the end. The book would hardly have sold if they hadn't!

It wasn't just the Latinate analysis that proved to be a barrier. It was the kind of English that was being presented: the usage of the best authors – 'the wells of English undefiled,' as Dr Johnson put it in the preface to his *Dictionary*. There was nothing wrong with that in itself, of course, but when it came to illustrating how English grammar works it presented a problem, as the illustrative sentences were often long and complex. Here's an example from the way Murray introduced the rule that two singular nouns, coordinated as a subject, have the verb agreeing with them in the plural. This can be illustrated quite simply with a sentence such as *The boy and the girl are in the garden*, where the verb has to be *are* and not *is*. But he illustrates the rule with this monster:

The sun that rolls over our heads, the food that we receive, the rest that we enjoy, daily *admonish* us of a superior and superintending Power.

The example makes the point, but the presence of so much extra syntactic complexity obscures it. No glamour here.
Anyone studying English grammar does ultimately need to

make contact with the usage of the best authors, for that will demonstrate the expressive excellence that can be achieved in the language – but surely not at the outset, during the first steps in engaging with the subject. Here, we need an approach tuned to the interests and needs of the learners, in which the grammar of speech is analysed along with the grammar of writing, and examples are chosen to which they can easily relate. Above all, the examples need to be real, not artificial – a reflection of the way language is actually used. This is where the glamour lies, as we'll see in Chapter 16.

Keyword: prescriptive

The term *prescriptive* was introduced by linguists in the 1930s to characterize the approach of the eighteenth-century grammarians, which during the Victorian era led to the publication of many more grammars and continued to be the dominant influence on grammar teaching in schools until the mid-twentieth century. It wasn't the Latinate description that motivated the term, nor the concentration on a formal written style, but the way the approach was used to control how people spoke and wrote in their daily lives.

A *prescriptive grammar* is one that lays down rules to which all usage must conform. Now if those rules are based on how the language actually works, there isn't an issue. If I'm teaching English as a foreign language, and I tell my students that they must put the definite article before the noun, then I am being prescriptive, but rightly so, for this is a genuine rule of the language to which all speakers and writers conform. What upset so many people, from the eighteenth century onwards – and what continues to upset people today – is that the prescriptions made by Murray and the others were often not genuine rules. People were being advised to speak and write in ways that bore little relation to English linguistic reality.

Some of the prescriptions (what you must do) and proscriptions (what you mustn't do) have become very well known, their unreal status having attracted the attention of satirists and usage commentators for nearly 200 years. The one I used in my introduction is a famous example: never end a sentence with a preposition (as in *This is the man I was talking to*). The anxiety seems to have originated in the poet John Dryden, who found such sentence-endings rhythmically weak and a departure from the kind of stylistic elegance he associated with Latin, where prepositions, as their name implied, went 'before'. The grammarians took up the point and developed it. Here is what Robert Lowth has to say:

> This is an idiom, which our language is strongly inclined to: it prevails in common conversation, and suits very well the familiar style in writing: but the placing of the preposition before the Relative is more graceful, as well as more perspicuous; and agrees much better with the solemn and elevated style.

No linguist would argue with the first and last parts of his sentence: the difference between the two constructions is indeed one of formality. *This is the man I was talking to* is much more informal ('familiar') than *This is the man to whom I was talking*. If the grammarians had gone on to recognize this variation, and recommend that both be used in their appropriate circumstances, informal and formal, a huge amount of later argument would have been avoided. Winston Churchill would never have needed to make the famous remark attributed to him that a clumsy avoidance of end-placed prepositions is 'the sort of English up with which I will not put'.

But that is not what the prescriptivists did. The tradition

that evolved was one that disapproved of variety, and condemned it. Lowth, as Murray after him, wanted only the formal alternative to be used: we should *never* end a sentence with a preposition – or (adds Murray) with 'any inconsiderable word'. No matter that Shakespeare, among other great writers, used both constructions. Lowth includes as examples of bad usage *Who servest thou under?* (from *Henry V*), and *Who do you speak to?* (from *As You Like It*). Clearly, if even Shakespeare can get it wrong, there is little hope for the rest of us – unless, of course, we follow the prescriptions of the grammarians.

Few people would be in sympathy with this mindset today, but in the eighteenth century it was widely accepted, as part of the need to maintain a clear identity among those who were members of the country's social elite, or who wished to become part of it. To be a member of 'polite' society meant conforming to the rules of etiquette, conduct, and courtesy that defined gentility and good breeding. All aspects of behaviour were involved, with a polished, elegant, and correct use of language considered to be of prime importance. And who would decide what was correct? It was accepted that it would be those who wrote the grammars, dictionaries, and pronunciation manuals.

Today it's difficult to appreciate the level of respect that was given to the individual writers on language. One quotation sums up the prevailing attitude of the time. In 1754 Lord Chesterfield wrote a letter to *The World* about Dr Johnson's forthcoming Dictionary (which included an outline of English grammar). We must choose, he says, a 'dictator' to rid the language of the chaos into which it has fallen:

> I give my vote for Mr Johnson to fill that great and arduous post. And I hereby declare that I make a total surrender

of all my rights and privileges in the English language, as
a freeborn British subject, to the said Mr Johnson, during
the term of his dictatorship. Nay more; I will not only obey
him, like an old Roman, as my dictator, but, like a modern
Roman, I will implicitly believe in him as my pope, and hold
him to be infallible while in the chair; but no longer.

I can't imagine this level of subservience being acceptable
nowadays, other than by a few prescriptively minded usage
pundits, each of whom would claim they were eminently
suited for such a role.

What this meant was that educated people following the
prescriptive approach would do their best never to place a
preposition at the end of a sentence, split an infinitive (*to
boldly go*), separate *only* from the word it modifies (*I only
bought tomatoes*), use *they* to refer to a singular pronoun
(*anyone who wants their tickets ...*), choose *between* rather than
among for more than two entities (*I have to decide between three
courses of action*), and take on board a few dozen other rules
in order to make their speech and writing socially acceptable.
The reasoning behind some of these rules now strikes us as
bizarre. Take one of Murray's violations of the rule governing
the choice of relative pronoun (as in *the man who/whose/whom
... vs the train that/which ...*):

> We hardly consider little children as persons, because
> that term gives us the idea of reason and reflection: and
> therefore the application of the personal relative *who*, in this
> case, seems to be harsh.

So we must never say *The child who ...*

We can see from that example how prescriptive grammatical decisions reflect far more than purely linguistic consider-
ations: it is influenced by the beliefs, attitudes, and tastes that

comprise someone's world view. Why is the mid-placed preposition desirable? Lowth's claim that it is 'more perspicuous' is plainly false, as the two sentences mean exactly the same thing, and neither version is any more or less clear than the other. The real reason is that he thinks it is 'more graceful', which is a personal aesthetic response that places grammar on the same level as choices of hairstyle and clothing.

Despite the early criticisms by writers such as Hazlitt, it took over a century before the weaknesses in the prescriptivist position came to be widely appreciated, and an alternative approach evolved. The reason it took so long is that the arguments had a seductive initial plausibility. One construction was claimed to be clearer, more precise, more elegant, or more natural than the other. Everyone, of course, wants to be clear and precise, but it took a while before it dawned on educators that prescriptive rules do not actually add extra clarity or precision. On the contrary, they go against these values by introducing a self-conscious stylistic awkwardness that actually makes it more difficult to grasp the meaning of what is being said. When people say such things as *boldly to go*, departing from the natural rhythm of the language, or ignore context by insisting on *I bought only tomatoes*, they hinder rather than help the process of comprehension.

There are indeed grammatical principles that make one sentence construction easier to understand than another, and these came to light as a result of the alternative view of grammar that developed in the twentieth century, as part of the new science of linguistics.

Interlude: *A shocking faux pas*

A CASE FOR LINDLEY MURRAY.

Cook (who is not in the best of Humours). *" Don't bother! No, I don't want none!"*
Boy. *" Well, leastways, you might ha' spoke Grammer!"*

A typical piece of Punch *grammatical satire,*
from volume 34, 1858, p. 222

English grammar, according to Lindley Murray in the opening sentence of his book, is 'the art of speaking and writing the English language with propriety'. The notion of a 'proper' English, as defined by the grammars, acceptable to high society, coloured the way the subject was taught in schools in the nineteenth century, and left an elitist legacy that is still with us. The writers in *Punch* magazine regularly poured scorn on what they saw to be the more arrogant prescriptions, as in this article from the issue of 5 March 1898.

The Latest Thing In Crime
(*A Dialogue of the Present Day*)

SCENE – Mrs. Featherstone's Drawing-room. Mrs.
Thistledown discovered calling.

Mrs. Thistledown (taking up a novel on a side-table). 'The
Romance of a Plumber,' by Paul Poshley. My dear Flossie,
you *don't* mean to tell me you read *that* man?
Mrs. Featherstone. I haven't had time to do more than dip
into it as yet. But why, Ida? *Oughtn't* I to read him?
Ida. Well, from something Mr. Pinceney told me the other
day – but really it's too bad to repeat such things. One never
knows, there *may* be nothing in it.
Flossie. Still, you might just as well *tell* me, Ida! Of course I
should never dream –
Ida. After all, I don't suppose there's any secret about it. It
seems, from what Mr. Pinceney says, that this Mr. Poshley
– you must *promise* not to say I told you –
Flossie. Of course – of course. But do go on, Ida. What does
Mr. Poshley do?
Ida. Well, it appears he *splits his infinitives.*
Flossie (horrified). Oh, not *really*! But how *cruel* of him! Why, I
met him at the Dragnetts' only last week, and he didn't look
at *all* that kind of person!
Ida. I'm afraid there's no doubt about it. It's perfectly
notorious. And of course any one who once takes to *that* –
Flossie. Yes, indeed. *Quite* hopeless. At least, I *suppose* so.
Isn't it?
Ida. Mr. Pinceney seemed to think so.
Flossie. How sad! But can't anything be *done*, Ida? Isn't there
any law to punish him? By the bye, how do you split – what
is it? – infinitudes?
Ida. My dear, I thought you knew. I really didn't like to ask
any questions.

Flossie. Well, whatever it is, I shall tell Mudies not to send me anything more of his. I *don't* think one ought to encourage such persons.

13

Clarity and weight

The way grammar contributes to clarity was gradually coming to be understood in linguistics, during the second half of the twentieth century, thanks to the emergence of the field of psycholinguistics. Psycholinguists explore the relationship between language and the properties of mind, such as attention, memory, and intelligence, and notions such as clarity and ambiguity are part of that. The study of the way children acquire language formed one branch of the subject ('developmental psycholinguistics'). Another was the study of the mental processes underlying the planning, production, perception, and comprehension of spoken and written language.

This complemented the approach of the big descriptive grammars, intent on demonstrating the system underlying the way sentences were constructed. Putting it crudely: the larger a sentence, the greater the task of comprehension, and the greater the need for clarity. Traditional grammar often reduced the notion of clarity to a focus on individual words, such as insisting that *only* should go next to the word it qualifies (*We saw only one performance*, rather than *We only saw ...*) or that a singular verb should be used after *none* (*None of the books is expensive*, rather than *... are expensive*). In fact, ambiguity arising out of such alternatives is extremely rare, and often non-existent. The choice between *we was* and *we were* has nothing to do with clarity: both are equally clear, though one usage is standard and the other nonstandard. Nor does the choice between *who* and *whom, different from* and *different to,* and most of the other shibboleths that have exercised grammatical purists. The real factors governing clarity lie elsewhere.

Keyword: weight

Say the following two sentences aloud. Which of them is more natural and easier to understand?

> It was nice of John and Mary to come and visit us the other day.
> For John and Mary to come and visit us the other day was nice.

I've tested sentence pairs like this many times, and never come across anyone who prefers the second sentence. People say things like it's 'awkward' and 'clumsy'; 'ending the sentence with *was nice* sounds abrupt'; 'putting all that information at the beginning stops me getting to the point'; and 'the first one's much clearer'.

Here's another example. Which of these two sentences sounds more natural?

> The trouble began suddenly on the thirty-first of October 1998.
> The trouble began on the thirty-first of October 1998 suddenly.

Again, the first is judged to be the better alternative. The second sentence doesn't break any grammatical rules, and could easily turn up in a novel, but few people like it, and some teachers would correct it.

What both these examples show is the importance of length, or *weight.* The first pair illustrates how English speakers like to place the 'heavier' part of a sentence towards the end rather than at the beginning. The second pair shows a preference for a longer time adverbial to come after a shorter one. Both illustrate the principle of *end-weight*. It was a principle that the prescriptive grammarians recognized too. In his appendix on 'perspicuity', Lindley Murray states several rules for promoting what he calls the 'strength' of sentences. His fourth rule is: 'when our sentence consists of two members, the longer should, generally, be the concluding one'.

Children learn this principle early in their third year of life. Suzie, for example, knew the phrase *red car*, and around age two started to use it in bigger sentences, as described in Chapter 4. But she would say such things as *see red car* long before she said things like *red car gone*. In grammatical terms: she expanded her object before she expanded her subject.

It will be that way throughout her life. Adults too in their conversational speech keep their subjects short and put the bulk of the information after the verb. Three-quarters of the clauses we use in everyday conversation begin with just a pronoun or a very short noun phrase:

<u>I</u> know what you're thinking.
<u>We</u> went to the show by taxi.
<u>The rain</u> was coming down in buckets.

Only as speech becomes more formal and subject matter more intricate do we encounter long subjects:

<u>All the critical remarks that have been made about his conduct</u> amount to very little.

Taking in such a sentence, we feel the extra demand being made on our memory. We have to keep those eleven words in mind before we learn what the speaker or writer is going to do to them.

Longer subjects, of course, are common in written English, as in this science report:

> The products of the decomposition of diaryl peroxides in various solvents have been extensively studied by Smith (1992).

A really long subject, especially one containing difficult words or concepts, may make such a demand on our working memory that we have to go back and read the sentence again, as in this tax-return instruction from the 1960s:

> Particulars of the date of sale and sale price of a car used only for the purposes of your office or employment (or the date of cessation of use and open market price of that date) should be furnished on a separate sheet.

This is the kind of sentence up with which the Plain English Campaign did not put. And indeed, as a result of that campaign, tax returns and other documents for public use have had a serious linguistic makeover in recent years.

In speech, if a subject goes on for too long, listener frustration starts to build up, as it's difficult to retain all the information without knowing what's going to be done with it:

> My supporters in the party, who have been behind me from the very outset of this campaign, and who know very well that the country is also behind me, ...

We urgently need a verb! It's a problem that can present itself in writing too, as when we read a slowly scrolling news headline on our television screen that begins like this:

> The writer and broadcaster John Jones, author of the best-selling series of children's books on elephants, and

well-known presenter of natural history programmes on BBC2, ...

... has won a prize? Has died? Has joined Real Madrid? Once, the scrolling subject went on for so long that I had forgotten the name of the person by the time the sentence came to an end, announcing his death.

Long subjects can be a problem for children in their early reading. The sooner they get to the verb, the sooner they will get a sense of what the sentence is about. So a sentence such as this one presents an immediate processing difficulty:

A big red jug full of warm milk was on the table.

Eight words to hold in mind before we get to the point. The end-weight principle suggests it would be easier to read as:

On the table was a big red jug full of warm milk.

So, writers of children's readers should avoid long subjects wherever possible, at least in the early stages. And children who competently handle long subjects in their writing should receive due credit for it. But I've never seen curriculum materials that recognize what has been achieved through mastering the principle of end-weight.

This is just one of several grammatical principles brought to light by the descriptive approach to grammar. I'll present another in the next chapter. Their importance is that these are the kind of factors that do truly determine clarity in language, and they ought to be given a prominent place in teaching materials. But I wonder, if we took a poll of teachers, how many would have come across the end-weight principle, and how many would have made it a part of their routine work on grammar? I suspect that there are still several important areas of 'knowledge about grammar' that have not yet left the descriptive handbooks and entered the classroom.

Interlude: Redistributing weight

Crystal Mark 21526
Clarity approved by
Plain English Campaign

On the website of the UK's Plain English Campaign there are several examples of 'before and after' – an obscure piece of English rewritten to make clear what it is saying. One of the examples is an excellent illustration of the way long subjects contribute to the overall difficulty of a text. The subject in each of the three clauses is in italics.

> *Your enquiry about the use of the entrance area at the library for the purpose of displaying posters and leaflets about Welfare and Supplementary Benefit rights*, gives rise to the question of the provenance and authoritativeness of the material to be displayed. *Posters and leaflets issued by the Central Office of Information, the Department of Health and Social Security and other authoritative bodies* are usually displayed in libraries, but *items of a disputatious or polemic kind, whilst not necessarily excluded*, are considered individually.

In the first sentence, the writer seems to have sensed there was something wrong with the length, as a comma has been (wrongly) inserted at the end of the subject construction (*rights*), presumably to give both writer and reader a moment to take stock. Normally, modern English disallows a comma between a subject and a predicate.

The Plain English Campaign version gets to the point, eliminating all the detail:

Thank you for your letter asking for permission to put up posters in the library. Before we can give you an answer we will need to see a copy of the posters to make sure they won't offend anyone.

However, if you thought this too radical a solution, and wanted to keep all the vocabulary, the text is immediately clearer if the syntactic weight is redistributed. Again, the subjects are in italics.

> *We* have received your enquiry about the use of the entrance area at the library for the purpose of displaying posters and leaflets about Welfare and Supplementary Benefit rights. *This* gives rise to the question of the provenance and authoritativeness of the material to be displayed. *We* do usually display in libraries posters and leaflets issued by the Central Office of Information, the Department of Health and Social Security and other authoritative bodies, but *we* consider individually items of a disputatious or polemic kind, whilst not necessarily excluding them.

The Crystal Mark is the PEC's seal of approval for the clarity of a document. As of 2016, over 21,000 documents have been approved in this way, each with its own identification number (replacing the zeros in the above picture). I should add that the similarity between the Mark's name and my own is purely coincidental.

14
Clarity and order

One of the dangers in the usage trade is seeing everything in black and white terms.

Prescriptivism bad; descriptivism good. As my quotation from Lindley Murray in the previous chapter showed, there was a lot of good stylistic sense in the prescriptive tradition, which has been overshadowed by its constant reiteration of unauthentic grammatical rules. Much of his appendix on perspicuity could, with minor rephrasing, appear in any modern grammar.

Here's another of his rules for preserving the strength of a sentence:

> Attend particularly to the use of copulatives, relatives, and all the particles employed for transition and connexion.

He explains:

> These little words, *but, and, or, which, whose, where, then, therefore, because,* &c. are frequently the most important words of any; they are the joints or hinges upon which all sentences turn.

And here is one of his rules for promoting the unity of a sentence:

> Never to crowd into one sentence things which have so little connexion, that they could bear to be divided into two or three sentences.

This is his example of something going wrong:

> Archbishop Tillotson died in this year. He was exceedingly beloved by king William and queen Mary, who nominated Dr. Tennison, bishop of Lincoln, to succeed him.

He remarks:

> Who would expect the latter part of this sentence to follow in consequence of the former? 'He was exceedingly beloved by both king and queen', is the proposition of the sentence. We look for some proof of this, or at least something related to it to follow; when we are on a sudden carried off to a new proposition.

It is an eminently sensible principle, which English teachers would immediately identify with, having often seen such sentences in their pupils' writing as:

> We spent the last day on the beach, where we bought an ice cream and Daddy missed the train.

Teachers are often unsure what to do with a sentence like this, because no grammatical rules have actually been broken. It is a perfectly fine compound-complex sentence (p. 72). But as soon as we allow meaning into the equation, as we must, it's clear that something has gone wrong with the logic of the narrative. Only an approach which focuses on meaning can sort this out. Grammar, as we'll see in the next chapter, should never be divorced from meaning.

Keyword: order

Murray was very concerned about how clarity was affected by the way constructions were connected in sentences, and this emphasis on connectivity has become a major topic in present-day grammatical thinking. It's an important development in child language acquisition too, as we saw in Chapter 10.

To recap: when children approach their third birthday, they start stringing sentences together to tell stories, using their new-found discovery of the magical connective *and*. A closer analysis of these compound sentences shows that the narratives unfold in the simplest possible way:

A happened and then B happened and then C happened ...

There is a neat parallelism between the sequence of clauses and the sequence of events they describe: the first thing mentioned is the first thing that happened; the second thing mentioned is the second thing that happened; and so on.

The relationship between the two types of sequence is called *order-of-mention*. The basic order is the one used by the three-year-old, and once learned, it is never forgotten. It remains the commonest way of telling a story, as illustrated by this extract from one of the conversations about an unfortunate driving incident recorded for the Survey of English Usage (the slash marks represent the end of an intonation unit):

so she came out / very gingerly / and opened the door / and sat in the car / and began to back / very very gently / and as she backed / there was an unpleasant crunching sound / and she slapped on the brakes / and looked around frantically ...

The connecting words may vary, but the direction is the same: first the coming out, then the door opening, then the sitting down ...

If all stories were like this, life would get very dull, so

grammar gives people the opportunity to vary the order-of-mention, using conjunctions, adverbials, and other features. In this next example, the first thing that's mentioned is *not* the first thing that happens:

> Before the customers left the shop the security staff arrived.

Nor is it here:

> The security staff arrived after the customers left the shop.

Conjunctions such as *before* and *after* reverse the order-of-mention. So do some adverbials (often, with an accompanying change in the time reference of the verb):

> The customers left the shop. The security staff had <u>already</u> arrived.
> The customers left the shop. <u>Some minutes earlier</u>, the security staff had arrived.

The options for storytelling are now greatly increased, and speakers and writers regularly make use of them. Young children, too. Suzie was manipulating order-of-mention by the time she was three-and-a-half, with sentences like:

> I give teddy a drink after I give him a wash.

So do teachers. When Suzie gets to school she will hear many instructions that reverse order-of-mention:

> Now, before you go out to play, I want you to put your books away.

A not uncommon reaction, from a child who's not been listening carefully, or who is unclear about the reversative meaning of *before*, is to go out to play immediately. It's a common problem with children who have some form of grammatical disability, and also in dyslexia. They can handle the straightforward order-of-mention with *and*, but they find *before* constructions harder to process, and *after* constructions hardest of all.

> Put your books away and (then) go out to play.
> Before you go out to play, put your books away.
> Go out to play after you put your books away.

Variations of this kind become especially important when they start to interfere with comprehension. This is likely to happen when the clauses being linked are lengthy or contain critical information. Here's an example from a junior history book:

> In 1666 there was a great fire in London. The year before there had been a great plague. The fire destroyed the plague.

I remember observing a class when the teacher, having read aloud the relevant section, asked the children to tell her what happened. There was silence. 'What happened first?' she prompted. One child put his hand up: 'There was a fire.' 'And what happened next?' 'There was a plague.' 'But,' said the teacher, 'if the plague happened after the fire, how did the fire destroy the plague?' Silence. Then one child put up her hand: 'There must have been another fire.'

Evidently the reversing function of the phrase *the year before* had not been noticed or understood. Should the author have written more clearly for this age of child? It would certainly have been clearer to follow the basic order-of-mention:

> In 1665 there was a great plague in London. The next
> year there was a great fire. The fire destroyed the plague.

But a history writer might well argue: if a whole book were
written in this mechanical way, wouldn't it become very
boring? And a teacher might well argue: surely it's good for
children to be exposed to more challenging grammatical constructions, for how else will they learn?

Clarity is a tricky concept, as it always raises issues of level
and audience. What scientists write in a technical journal
will be clear to their colleagues, but unclear to non-special-
ists. That was what prompted the Plain English Campaign: to
draw attention to writing that failed to appreciate the needs
of readers by using grammar (and vocabulary) that is difficult
to understand. Writers for children also have to be aware of
the grammatical level that their readers have reached. For
example, if children are still having difficulty handling the
distinction between active and passive in their speaking and
listening (p. 81), it would be unwise to put passive constructions into their early readers, and unrealistic to expect them
to use passives in their early writing.

The four modes of communication are interdependent. It's
long been recognized that writing depends on reading, and
that speaking depends on listening. Now all four modes form
a chain: 'writing depends on reading … depends on speaking
… depends on listening'. The novelty is to draw attention to
the link between reading and speaking – between literacy and
oracy. Every point in grammar needs to be considered from
all four points of view.

Often, a grammatical difficulty is first noted in written
work. For example, when children first start to write stories,
they tend to overuse the word *and*. Here's a typical instance
from a seven-year-old's account of an imaginary wedding:

> I wore a long white dress and I wore a pretty veil and I
> picked some flowers from the garden and I put them on
> my dress ...

How might this be improved? There are, of course, many
ways, but when I used this extract with a group of primary
teachers and asked them how they would improve it, while
keeping as closely as possible to the original, virtually all of
them split the above example into two, and several corrected
the order-of-mention. Here's one response:

> I wore a long white dress and a pretty veil. During the
> morning I had picked some flowers from the garden and
> put them on my dress ...

Asked how they would work further on this, most reckoned
that it would be useful to collect a number of connective
words and phrases, understandable by a seven-year-old in
everyday speech, that could be practised in contexts like this
one. Within five minutes, they had put together a list of over
twenty time expressions, such as *earlier, the day before,* and
before lunch. Some added expressions to the list that would
take the story in a different direction, such as *unfortunately*
and *luckily.*

They then explored which of these expressions the children would be likely to encounter in their reading at that
age. It didn't take them long to find examples of shifts in
time perspective in the books on their shelves, such as this
one from the old Ape's story in Roderick Hunt's *My Home*
(Oxford Reading Tree):

> In this jungle my song is sung.
> Once I was strong.

Or this one, from Michael Bond's *Paddington at Large*:

> Before Paddington had time to open his mouth Mr Curry
> produced a saw and a length of rope ...

They agreed that drawing attention to the way these writers
tell their stories would help children develop a stronger sense
of how order-of-mention works and – with some authors
already becoming favourites – give them additional motiv-
ation to try using the more mature alternatives themselves.

As with end-weight, order-of-mention is an important
grammatical principle that is central to many uses of language. It influences the character not only of literary narrative but also of such everyday genres as instructions and
sports commentary. Anyone who has thrown a set of instructions on the ground in disgust at their lack of clarity will
know how badly they can be phrased, and upon inspection it
often transpires that one of the grammatical culprits is poor
order-of-mention. The following is a real example:

1. Take the four screws P and use them to join the top of
   struts A and B.
2. Take the four screws Q and use them to join the base
   of struts A and B.
3. A washer G should be used with each screw before
   use.

Yet, despite its high frequency of use and its relevance for
clarity, the order-of-mention principle is noticeably absent
from the way grammar is described in curriculum materials.
It's another example of the gap that still remains between
theory and practice.

15

Grammar and meaning

Notions such as accuracy, precision, clarity, and the avoidance of ambiguity are what we want our children to learn about grammar, and how we want to be able to use grammar ourselves. They have one thing in common: they are all to do with the expression of meaning. Meaning is at the heart of everything we want children (and adults) to do in their interactions. Speakers and writers need to express their meaning clearly and precisely, and listeners and readers need to understand the meaning of those communicating with them. The emphasis was captured very nicely in the title of a book by Michael Halliday on child language development: *Learning How to Mean* (1977).

However, most people don't immediately associate meaning with grammar, but with vocabulary. The more 'word power' we have, it is said (and I'm now recalling the famous column in *Reader's Digest*, 'It pays to increase your word power'), the better we will be able to express what we mean. That is why people use dictionaries: in principle, they contain all the meanings of all the words in a language. But words by themselves are not enough for meaningful communication. As we saw with Suzie's use of *push* in the introduction, a word by itself may have meaning, but it will not always make sense. For that to happen it needs to be put into a sentence. It needs grammar.

This is because the vast majority of words in English are

inherently ambiguous: we look them up in a dictionary and find they have more than one meaning (they are *polysemous*). *Charge* can be something to do with money, energy, or military activity (to name just three of its meanings). Some words have over a dozen meanings. A common verb such as *take* or *do* might have several dozen. How can we use language meaningfully when there is so much polysemy?

The answer, of course, is that grammar sorts it out. By putting words into a sentence, we combine them in ways that enable us to select just one of those meanings:

> The theatre charged for the tickets.
> The cavalry charged along the valley.
> I charged the battery in my phone.

The ambiguity has disappeared. The sentences have created sense out of the words they contain.

That is what sentences are for: to make sense of words. And that is what every grammatical construction is for – from the largest sentence patterns to the smallest word inflections: they are there to help us, literally, to make – construct, create – sense. There are over 3,500 index entries to the various features explained in the biggest descriptive grammar to come out of the twentieth century: *A Comprehensive Grammar of the English Language*, published in 1985. Each one is there for a reason: to help us express an aspect of our thinking in a way that others will understand. And because our thoughts are often complex, grammar is complex too. If all we ever wanted to say was at the level of 'Me Jane; you Tarzan', grammar would be easy.

What this amounts to is that grammar should never be studied or taught divorced from the meaning that the sentence patterns convey. To teach grammar without reference to meaning is the strategy that has given grammar a bad name. Anyone who has ever felt that grammar is boring, dull, pointless, and irrelevant has almost certainly been taught it in this way.

I was taught it like that. The teacher would put a sentence on the board (*The man sat on a chair*) and engage me in a dialogue that went something like this. I was aged about eleven or twelve at the time.

> Teacher: Can you name the two parts of this sentence, Crystal?
> Me: *The man* is the subject and *sat on a chair* is the predicate.
> Teacher: Good, and what's the most important word in the predicate?
> Me: *Sat*, sir.
> Teacher: Which is called ...?
> Me: The verb, sir.
> Teacher: Good boy. And what is *on a chair*?
> Me: The object, sir.
> Teacher: Crystal, Crystal, Crystal ... It is not an object. Does anyone else know what it is?
> [*silence*]
> Teacher: Have you all forgotten the lesson we had about adverb phrases?
> [*more silence*]
> Teacher: It's an adverb phrase of place. [*pause*] Can anyone tell me any other kinds of adverb phrase?

And that led to more silence, which meant that we all had to write out ten times the names of all the adverb phrases in English – of time, place, concession, result, and so on – with an example of each.

I remember thinking – but never having the courage to ask – 'why are we doing this?' And today I know the three kinds of answer that would have been given:

- Because (Crystal) the analysis of grammar has had a long and revered history that dates back to Plato, Aristotle, and the Stoics, and what was good enough for Plato should be good enough for you, so you will write out one hundred times ...
- Because when you learn to analyse sentences you will become a better user of your language – a better listener, speaker, reader, and writer.
- Because this will teach you the terms you will need when you start learning a foreign language.

None of these answers helped eliminate the boredom. The first was intellectually respectable, as part of the study of the history of ideas, but perhaps not a very relevant response for an eleven-year-old. The second might or might not have been true (see p. 253), but it was difficult to see such analyses producing any immediate benefit. And the third was an offer of manna to feed in a future French-language heaven, which sounded like a good idea – but was it worth making the present English class a mother-tongue purgatory?

To this day I have no idea why those early grammatical experiences didn't put me off grammar for life, as they did so many others. Probably, deep down, it was a predilection for analysing things. (I liked jigsaw puzzles too.) But I do clearly remember the day at university when in a lecture I understood for the first time what grammar analysis was really about, and in so doing learned the term *semantics*.

Keyword: semantics

Semantics is the study of the way meaning is conveyed in language. It is thus a very wide-ranging subject, including everything that could possibly contribute to the meaning of a piece of spoken or written language, such as vocabulary, discourse, intonation and tone of voice (in speech), punctuation and typography (in writing), and (in both speech and writing) grammar. A semantic perspective asks, of any linguistic feature: what does it mean? Or, what is its contribution to the overall meaning of what is being said or written?

With grammar, sometimes the meaning of a grammatical contrast is straightforward and easily stated, as in the two-way contrast in nouns between singular and plural described in Chapter 5, where the meaning is 'one' vs 'more than one'. With other grammatical features, the meaning is more difficult to state, especially when more than two contrasts are involved, as in the way verb forms divide up our sense of time into the different time zones traditionally called tenses: *I walk, I walked, I have walked, I had walked* ... But in all cases, some sort of meaning is there, waiting to be explained.

The contrast between active and passive constructions, already outlined in relation to child development (p. 81), is an interesting case in point. My old grammar-school teacher would have parsed these two types of sentence in this way (I explained the terminology in Chapter 8):

active: *the cat*   *chased*   *the mouse*
    SUBJECT VERB   OBJECT

passive: *the mouse* *was chased* *by the cat*
    SUBJECT VERB   ADVERBIAL [an Agent]

Having done that, with a few more examples, he would have felt his job was done. His students would recognize a passive sentence when they saw one, and might conceivably use one in their own writing. Certainly, they would be able to answer one of the questions in the English-language exam, which might be: 'Read the following paragraph and identify every sentence containing a passive verb'. You could get 100 per cent for a question like that – without ever needing to know what the difference between active and passive means.

The grammar class is over when you've parsed the sentence? The semantic approach says no: it is only just beginning. And a semantic analysis of the contrast between active and passive immediately brings to light an unusual result: in this particular case, there seems to be no difference of meaning. The two sentences are synonymous: *the mouse chased the cat = the cat was chased by the mouse*. This immediately raises the question: why? What is the point in a language having two ways of saying the same thing? It seems an unnecessary luxury. We would expect one or other of the ways to have died out over time; but both active and passive are alive and well in present-day English.

One of the insights of descriptive grammar is not just to analyse the elements of a sentence, but also to demonstrate what can be done with them. We saw this with adverbials (p. 64): to fully understand the grammar of the sentence *Forcefully, Chris kicked the ball*, we need to know what word-order variations are possible. We should be aware that the adverbial can move about the sentence (as in *Chris forcefully kicked the ball* and *Chris kicked the ball forcefully*). We should also be aware that the subject and object are obligatory: we can't leave one out and say *Forcefully, kicked the ball* or *Forcefully, Chris kicked*. This is all part of our 'knowledge about grammar'.

So, what knowledge of this kind do we have in relation to active and passive constructions? One point is critical. In the active sentence, the element after the verb (the object) is obligatory: we cannot say *the cat chased*. But in the passive sentence, the element after the verb (the agent) is optional: we *can* say *the mouse was chased*. Putting this in semantic terms: in an active sentence, we are forced to say 'who did it'; in a passive sentence, we aren't.

In grammar, one question always leads to another. Why would we ever want to say that something happened, without wanting to say 'who did it'? To answer this, we need to explore yet another dimension of language, also essential if grammar is to come alive. And it is here that we will find the long-awaited holy grail of grammatical glamour.

Interlude: Real and unreal ambiguity

We need to avoid ambiguity when speaking or writing – unless, of course, we deliberately want our words to be taken in more than one way, as happens in jokes, puns, and a great deal of poetry. Grammar lies at the heart of many inadvertent ambiguities, as illustrated by these examples from W. H. Mittins, *A Grammar of Modern English* – a pioneering book in its day (1962) for its common-sense approach. Identifying the places in a sentence where ambiguities often arise is a major help towards avoiding them.

Is it a noun or a verb – as in these newspaper headlines?
Giant waves down funnel.
Fresh herrings plan to beat slump.

Is it a compound noun or a verb?
She liked stewing steak.
They asked questions about my spending money.

Where should the prepositional phrase go?
The police were searching for clues to the murder with a magnifying glass.
He could see the workers pulling down the pigsty from the roof.
The fire was put out before any damage could be done by the fire brigade.

Where should the 'that' conjunction go?
He said before leaving he would answer all the letters.
She told me when she finished her studies she would marry me.
The actor admitted without prompting he would never have remembered his lines.

What is the 'and' conjunction linking?
The only spectators were a woman carrying a small baby
and a large policeman.
All old men and women ought to be evacuated from the
danger area.
He had a large collection of illustrated magazines and
books.

The famous 'dangling participles' – at beginning or end
On failing the entrance examination, his father sent him
to a boarding school.
Covered with grease, the water did not seem unduly cold
to the swimmer.
We saw the Eiffel Tower flying from London to Paris.
I bought a book about an escape from a prison camp
called 'The Wooden Horse'.

The problem isn't always one of clarity. There's no risk of
misunderstanding with many dangling participles, because
our knowledge of the real world tells us how things are. The
Eiffel Tower example is a joke rather than an intelligibility
problem, for we all know that the Eiffel Tower can't fly. But
an unintended joke presents a problem of a different kind. It
can distract the listener or reader from what's being said, and
can introduce a laugh where one wouldn't be appropriate. I
don't know whether Mittins' example of a memorial inscrip-
tion was genuine, but I can imagine the embarrassment if it
was:

Erected to the Memory of George Baker
Drowned in the Thames by his Fellow Directors

16

Grammar and effect

Government reports into the teaching of English, in any country, usually contain statements like this:

> We take it as axiomatic that a primary objective of the educational system must be to enable and encourage every child to use the English language to the fullest effect in speaking, writing, listening and reading.

(That one was from the UK's Kingman Report of 1988.) If I had a pound for every time *effect* and its variants (*effective, ~ly, ~ness*) turned up in government reports on English, I would be a very well-off linguist indeed. The usage even outnumbers the use of *mean* and its variants. The word was never explained: it was simply assumed that everyone knew what an effective use of language was – just as everyone was supposed to know what a clear or precise use of language was.

For decades, linguists made the same assumption. It was only in the 1970s that they realized the question of effect demanded just as much investigation as any other aspect of communication, and only in the 1980s that the first books began to appear offering tentative answers as part of a new branch of linguistics. It was called *pragmatics*.

The term was new in a linguistic context, but its etymology was familiar, as people use the word *pragmatic* in everyday life. If I say that *John is a very pragmatic person*, I mean he adapts his behaviour to meet the needs of the situation in which he finds himself. In situation X he chooses to behave in one way; in situation Y he chooses to behave in another. The opposite of pragmatic is *dogmatic*, or perhaps *principled*. If I say that *John is a very dogmatic person*, I mean he *always* behaves in a certain way, regardless of the circumstances. He doesn't need to choose, because his principles dictate his behaviour.

The common element is 'choice', and this became the defining notion in the way linguists began to explore the domain of pragmatics. All aspects of language were affected: choices in vocabulary, pronunciation, punctuation, spelling – and grammar. The subject was of immediate interest to parents and teachers, because it reflected the kind of decision-making the children were involved in every day. A correction, whether at home or in class, is basically the recommendation of an alternative choice. It draws attention to the options that the language makes available to them as speakers, writers, listeners, and readers.

Keyword: pragmatics

Pragmatics is the study of the choices we make when we use language, the reasons for those choices, and the effects that those choices convey. When linguists started to investigate pragmatics, they approached it from different angles. Some focused on the choices themselves; some on the intentions behind the choices; some on the results of the choices. Text-book introductions to pragmatics can look very different, as a result. But they all have one aim: to *explain* the choices that are made. In a word: they all want to answer the question 'why?'

As soon as we apply this perspective to the active/ passive distinction, we see the illumination that a pragmatic approach can provide. And the interest. For this is where grammar leaves the classroom and enters the real world – a world of dramatic headlines, prohibitions, experiments, social responsibilities, house decorators, hairdressers ... As soon as we ask 'Why would you ever want to use a passive construction without an agent?' – or, thinking semantically, 'Why would you ever want to say that something happened without wanting to say who did it?' – we enter that world.

So, as Michael Rosen might have said, 'We're going on a passive hunt. We're going to catch a big one ...' Having learned to identify passives, using the traditional technique described in the previous chapter, the game now is to look around to find examples of their use where the agent is omitted, around the school, at home, in the street.

They're not difficult to spot. We pass a newsagent, and on the billboard outside is the headline:

20 KILLED

It's a shortened form of the sentence '20 people have been killed'. And it's an agentless passive. Our curiosity is aroused. We go into the shop and buy the paper, and learn about the agent: 'Twenty people were killed by a tornado that struck ...' The headline writer knows very well not to give too much information away at the outset. If the billboard had said '20 killed by tornado', spelling out the agent, would we have bought the paper? As we now know the answer, it is less likely. Deliberately leaving a sentence unclear is a common headline-writing strategy, and the agentless passive is the ideal way of achieving this aim.

A little further down the street we see a sign:

ENTRY PROHIBITED

Another excellent passive without an agent. This one raises a different issue: who has made the prohibition? Is it the government, the owner, some individual? Does the prohibitor not want to say? If the authorizing agency is known, why is it not named? Why do such notices never appear in the active grammatical form? We never see: 'The government prohibits you' or 'We prohibit you', and the like. Is it because the use of the passive makes the command seem more impersonal, and thus more authoritative? I've sat in on school groups where these questions have been enthusiastically debated. Note: enthusiastically. About grammar.

Let's change the setting, and move around the school – into the science lab. Now a report of an experiment has to be written up. What should the budding scientist write? There are several options. Which of the following are desirable, which not? Which is the most appropriate use, and why?

> I mixed X and Y to produce Z.
> We mixed X and Y to produce Z.
> Our class mixed X and Y to produce Z.
> John and Mary mixed X and Y to produce Z.
> John, wearing a new red jumper, mixed X and Y to produce Z.
> X and Y were mixed to produce Z.

Another enthusiastic discussion. The red jumper example is quickly eliminated. Why? It's got nothing to do with the experiment. (Note that the teacher doesn't have to point this out: whenever I've heard students discuss this topic, they come up with the comment themselves.) But then, the argument continues, nor is it particularly relevant that it was John or Mary who mixed X and Y, because the result of the mixing would be the same whoever did it. 'I' and 'we' similarly personalize the account; and 'our class' does too. So what can we do if we want to avoid introducing any element of personal identity into our write-up? Is there a construction which allows us to say that something happened, without having to say who did it? The passive fills the bill. And that, presumably, is why it occurs so frequently in the objective, impersonal world we call science.

These are all examples from the written language. It's a bit trickier to go hunting for agentless passives in everyday speech, but they're certainly there, awaiting discovery. A good way of exploring them is to role-play situations where they would be used. Here are three examples:

- A teacher hears the sound of breaking glass outside the door. She goes to find out what has happened, and sees Michael on one side of a broken window and a football on the other. 'What happened, Michael?' she asks. Michael knows he has to say something relevant, and racks his brain for a construction that will, possibly, get him out of trouble – a construction that enables him to report that something happened without having to say who did it. 'The window's been broken, miss.' The passive as a means of evading responsibility. Unfortunately, the Kingman-inspired teacher is well aware of the functions of the passive, so the usage will not wash. 'Yes, I can see the window is broken, Michael, but who did it?' Give me an agent! Michael learns that grammar will not solve all his problems in life.
- Two acquaintances meet in the street, and they catch up with each other. 'Have you had your garage door replaced yet?' asks one. Evidently they've talked about this before. 'No, not yet,' says the other. And the conversation wanders off in other directions.

Here, an agent is unnecessary. It's not important to
the questioner to know who is going to be involved
in doing the replacing. The important thing is the
action, not the agent. In fact, it would suggest a very
different scenario if an agent had been mentioned:
'Have you had your garage door replaced by John
Smith yet?' That suggests that there is something
special in the history of this garage door – perhaps
John Smith made a mess of it first time around, or
perhaps John Smith garage doors are a must-have.
But with no such history, the passive allows the
question to be asked without loading it in any way.

- Two more acquaintances meet in the street, and
one explains why she's in this part of town: 'I've
just had my hair done.' The expected response will
be along the lines of 'It looks lovely.' A response
which questions the missing agent is dangerous:
'Really? Who by?' It all depends on the intonation
and facial expression, of course. With a tone and
face of enthusiastic admiration, the response is
flattering (implying: 'I'd like to have mine done by
that hairdresser too'). With an unemotional tone and
face, the response is the opposite (implying: 'I'd find
someone else, if I were you'). And, just as with the
garage situation, to spell out the agent at the outset
implies a special history: 'I've just had my hair done
by Tony' – who must be good, otherwise why bother
to mention him?

In all these cases, the pragmatic approach to grammar makes
us explore the reasons for using one or other of the options
English provides. The choice is simple: active vs passive,
agent mentioned or agent omitted. But the intentions behind

the choice can be complex, as can the effects that the choice conveys. Sometimes the two coincide: the speaker/writer's intention in using the agentless passive coincides with the effect it was hoped to have on the listener/reader. Sometimes, as in the case of poor Michael, it doesn't. But in all cases, we are a long way from the world of the grammar book and the blackboard. And to end by talking about hairdressers does show that grammar can, literally, lead us to glamour.

17
Structure and use together

The previous chapters make it clear that there are two sides to grammar. We hear and see actual sentences, and study how they are constructed using whatever terminology we can muster. I call that the dimension of *structure*. And we hear and see the circumstances in which the sentences are used, feel their effect, and judge their appropriateness to the situation. I call that the dimension of *use*.

The history of grammar shows – until very recently – each of these dimensions operating without the other. For centuries, people thought of grammar solely as structure – learning about parts of speech and parsing techniques – and paid negligible attention to how it was used, other than following the recommendations of prescriptive grammarians. Then, in the 1960s, the accumulated criticism of this approach by teachers, examiners, government advisory bodies, and the media led to the subject being dropped from the school curriculum around the English-speaking world. In Britain, the kiss of death came with the Secondary Schools Examination Council report of 1964, known as the Lockwood Report, which forthrightly condemned the grammar questions in the exams:

> We share the view that they are of doubtful utility in any
> examination of English language and that in their present
> form they do great harm. Such questions are often based
> on a few usages which are appropriate enough in some
> styles of language, but which have come to be traditionally

condemned as incorrect in all. Other exercises in the same class are based on traditionally prescribed rules of grammar which have been artificially imposed upon the language. They have had little relevance to usage at any past time and they have even less to contemporary usage.

The exams were dropped soon after, along with the teaching. And in the years that followed, a similar disaffection developed in the USA, Canada, Australia, New Zealand, and other English-speaking countries. Grammar was officially dead. A new generation of students would soon arise unaware of even the most basic technical notions, as my introductory story about prepositions and horses illustrated.

During the 1970s, the study of structure was widely replaced by the study of use. This was an approach in which students focused on the real-life situations in which language was used in distinctive ways, such as in newsreading, religious and legal settings, parliamentary reporting, advertising, and sports commentary. A class might collect a set of commercial advertisements, for example, and discuss what the ads were trying to do and how successful they were in doing it. They certainly ended up with a more critical view of the motives of advertisers; but there was very little discussion of the way in which the advertisements actually used language, other than some vague remarks about 'short sentences' and 'vivid words'. The reason was obvious: neither teacher nor student had any technical terms to help them do it.

We can get a sense of the problem through a comparison task. Try explaining the different dramatic effects between the following two sentences *without* using any grammatical terms.

The old, ruined house stood on the hillside.
The house, old, ruined, stood on the hillside.

You won't be able to do it comfortably and succinctly if you know nothing about grammar. But once you know how to use the terms *adjective* and *noun*, and are aware of the importance of word order, it's easy. Adjectives like *old* and *ruined* normally go before nouns in English; when they're used after a noun, with each one separately emphasized, the effect is immediately more atmospheric. In a lesson, having learned about the impact of this change in word order, it's then a simple matter to compile lists of adjectives and nouns, and try this rule out, to see if it always works. If it does, then – the teacher might continue – why not try using this kind of effect in a piece of story writing? Models can be found in books written by the students' favourite authors, to show that this isn't just an academic exercise. Here's one, from Terry Pratchett's *The Carpet People* (Chapter 13), in which Pismire saw 'the gleam of ten thousand eyes, green, red and white ...' A link between grammatical awareness and creative writing suggests itself.

Key phrase: two sides of a coin

The present-day trend in English grammar is to bring the two dimensions together: the 'two sides of a coin' approach. Structures are there to be used; and uses need structures in order to be fulfilled. We need to know how sentences are actually used if we are to make the study of grammar meaningful, rewarding, and – as suggested by its etymology – glamorous. If writing like Pratchett is an attractive goal, then seeing how he uses postposed adjectives will help writers move closer to that goal.

If structure and use aren't brought together, grammar becomes artificial and irrelevant, as these next examples show. I was reading a grammar book, written for students learning English as a foreign language, where the first chapter introduced a simple sentence: *This is a table*. There was a picture of a table. A list of other words was provided too, so students could practise saying *This is a chair*, *This is a door*, and so on. I've seen classes where each student in turn has to say such a sentence. The aim is clear: to get them to master the structure.

But from the 'use' point of view, there is a problem, for when in real life would we ever want to say *This is a table*? Do we enter a room, see a table, and expound to whoever is there, *This is a table*? We might, in some weird existentialist world. But such a sentence would never normally be used. The student is being taught something that is literally use-less.

It would only take a tweak to make it use-full. Add an adjective, and suddenly all kinds of real-life situations come to mind. I can easily imagine standing in a furniture shop and remarking *This is a well-made table*. Or in an antique shop listening to the owner telling me that *This is a genuine Venetian table*. We need some adjectives to make the sentences come alive.

Another example from foreign-language teaching. This time the pattern being drilled was *How old are you? I'm –*. The teacher asked the question, and the student had to reply with a real or fictitious age. Then each student asked the question of others in the class. After a few minutes, they were fluent in this interaction, and the teacher moved on to another construction.

Had they learned how to ask someone's age? From a structural point of view, yes. But from a 'language in use' point of view, not in the slightest. For when in real life do we ask people how old they are? The question is full of danger. There is suspicion, as when a shop-owner asks a young-looking, alcohol-buying customer 'How old are you?' in a belligerent tone of voice. There is warning, as when a doctor, having examined some test results, asks me, 'How old are you, Mr Crystal?', in a weary, I've-told-you-before-you-ought-to-do-more-exercise tone of voice. There is embarrassment, as when children ask adults how old they are – especially female adults. They learn that one of the things you *don't* do in life is go around blithely asking people their age.

Suzie learned that lesson at a birthday party. Granny was there, and – as adults tend to do – asked the birthday-child, as if she didn't know, 'How old are you today?' Suzie said 'four', and then added: 'And how old are you, Granny?' Laughter all round. 'Oh no, dear, you don't ask a lady her age.' It must be a puzzling moment. Why is the question all right going in one direction and not in the other? Suzie will learn that grammar is full of traps like that. One of the ways in which the study of grammar can be made intriguing is to explore them. And for this we need to see the interaction between structure and use.

This book is about English grammar, but the importance of bringing structure and use together can also be seen when learning other languages. When I was in school, the focus was entirely on structure. I remember learning about the difference between the two words for 'you' in French: *tu* was singular, addressing just one person; *vous* was plural, addressing more than one. It was different from present-day English, so the point was practised at length, with all the irregular verbs: *tu sais* ('you know') singular, *vous savez* plural.

Then I went to France for the first time, and in Paris, slightly lost, I saw a gendarme and tried out my French to ask the way. There was only one of him, so I used *tu*. *Monsieur*, I began, *tu sais où est ...?* ('you know where is ...?'). He looked at me very oddly. Only later did I learn what I did wrong: I had ignored the pragmatics of *tu* and *vous*. French adults would never use *tu* in such a situation. They use it to children, to animals, and to their intimates. From the gendarme's point of view, I was therefore either treating him as a child, or calling him a pig, or trying to get off with him. But my foreign accent and innocent demeanour presumably overruled any possible pragmatic offence.

Interlude: Define dog

Danish professor Otto Jespersen (1860–1943) has been described as 'the first descriptive grammarian'. In 1910, he wrote an article on 'Modern English grammar' for *The School Review*. Here are the opening two paragraphs.

A great many people seem to think that the study of grammar is a very dry subject indeed, but that it is extremely useful, assisting the pupils in writing and in speaking the language in question. Now I hold the exactly opposite view. I think that the study of grammar is really more or less useless, but that it is extremely fascinating. I don't think that the study of grammar, at least in the way in which grammar has been studied hitherto, has been of very material assistance to any one of the masters of English prose or poetry, but I think that there are a great many things in grammar that are interesting and that can be made interesting to any normal schoolboy or schoolgirl.

The chief thing is not to approach grammar from the side of logic or abstract definitions. What is wanted is to show that language is a living thing and what that means. When children begin to learn about cats and dogs they don't start with the definition of what a cat is or what a dog is, but they learn that this animal, which is very interesting to them, is a cat, and that this other animal, which is perhaps even more interesting to them, is a dog, and then perhaps after many years they will advance so far in their study of zoölogy that they would be asked in an examination the question: 'How would you define a cat?' or 'How would you define a dog?' – though I don't believe that even in the case of zoölogy you would think of asking that sort of question. Now, then, why should we start with definitions of nouns, adjectives, and verbs, and all these things? I don't see that there is any reason for that.

I take the middle road between Jespersen and traditional grammar. I think the study of grammar is both fascinating *and* useful. His caveat is noteworthy: 'at least in the way in which grammar has been studied hitherto'. That's the crucial point. In the century since he wrote, new methods have brought to light ways in which the study of grammar can indeed become useful in developing a child's (or adult's) ability to listen, speak, read, and write. There is glamour there, if we know how to find it.

18

A sense of style

How do we bring language structure and language use together? In my view, by bringing grammar into contact with semantics (which adds the perspective of meaning), and pragmatics (which adds the perspectives of intention and effect). Chapters 15 and 16 illustrated how this can be done, using the example of active and passive. But any topic in grammar can be approached in the same way.

It would take quite a large book to go through English grammar examining each feature from a semantic and pragmatic point of view. Even an introductory book illustrating the approach becomes lengthy, because as soon as an author begins to investigate the uses of a particular feature, the floodgates open: fascinating examples can be found in every area of human endeavour, and each is calling out 'Use me!' When I wrote in this way, back in 2004, in a book called *Making Sense of Grammar*, I reached 400 pages without difficulty, and the material I reluctantly put on one side would have doubled the size (and the price).

Even an apparently tiny point of grammar hides a multitude of uses. Take the word *we*. The traditional approach would simply say it is the first-person plural pronoun, and list it along with all the other pronouns. But that's just the beginning of the story of *we*.

The semantic approach would draw attention to the way *we* has alternative meanings, such as:

- the speaker/writer along with the person(s) being addressed: *I think we should leave now, John.*
- the speaker/writer without the person being addressed: *We can get there without your help.*
- the speaker/writer along with an indefinite number of others: *We won our last match* (i.e. the team plus supporters).
- the speaker/writer along with the rest of the world: *We aren't paying enough attention to climate change.*
- the speaker/writer alone, as in the 'royal *we*', very important when studying Shakespeare: *We are not amused.*

Especially important – and ignored in traditional accounts, which focused only on formal writing – are the cases where *we* refers to second and third persons:

- the speaker means the person being addressed, as with nurse to patient: *How are we today?*
- the speaker means some third person not present, as when two receptionists talk about the boss who has failed to greet them with a 'good morning': *We are in a nice mood today!*

The pragmatic approach asks *why* the word should be used in these various ways. What is the intention behind a carer who addresses a patient with *we*? And what is the effect of using it? For many, the usage is considered patronizing, and the resulting discomfort in the listener may not be what the speaker intended. A great deal of interesting discussion can arise from considering the simple contrast between *How are we today?* and *How are you today?* And other intriguing usages soon emerge, such as the police officer's *We don't want any trouble now, do we, sir?*

The investigation is not only interesting; it has practical outcomes, for we all have to make decisions about the use of *we* in our own writing. Should the style of an essay (story, letter, blog, email ...) be personal or not? The pragmatic choices include:

- the use of *I*, to convey a personal involvement: *I pointed out earlier ...*
- the use of *one*, to convey impersonal involvement: *One pointed out earlier ...*
- the use of *we*, to avoid an egotistical impression: *We pointed out earlier ...*
- the use of *we*, to suggest that writer and reader are involved in a joint enterprise (the 'authorial *we*'): *As we saw earlier ...*
- the use of *you*, which introduces a distance between writer and reader, and sometimes a hint of abruptness: *As you saw earlier ...*
- the use of *you*, meaning 'anyone', as an informal alternative to *one*: *You can see the beach from our house ...*
- avoiding all of these options, by using a passive: *It was pointed out earlier ...*

Once a decision is made, other semantic and pragmatic factors come into play, such as the need to avoid ambiguity and achieve consistency. Most people would find sequences such as the following unpalatable:

> We started the climb at six o'clock. You could see the summit clearly, and we thought it wouldn't take more than an hour to reach it. But one forgot about the mist, and I was surprised to find we were still a long way off at seven.

As other styles are explored, other techniques come to light, such as the replacement of a pronoun by some other construction. When a noun phrase replaces *I* or *you*, for instance, the effect is one of self-conscious formality:

> This reviewer has to say he has never seen such a terrible production.
> Readers of this column will not be surprised to learn ...

It's easy to see how, in a school, a whole lesson might be devoted to the way pronouns are used in English as part of the development of a pleasing personal or professional style.

Keyword: style

The semantic/pragmatic approach is, essentially, a replacement of 'what' questions by 'why' questions. Explanations are what make grammar interesting and exciting for everyone, as they bring grammar off the page and into the real world. They make us see that grammar is a dynamic, purposeful, thought-provoking activity which relates to all of us. It is a subject that can be applied to any and every use of language, past and present. Why did N use X in that way in that sentence? What would have happened if N hadn't used it, or used it in a different way, or replaced it with some other feature? For X, read passive, adjective, past tense, adverbial, subordinate clause, or any other feature of English grammar. For N, read politician, scientist, sports commentator, journalist, Shakespeare, or any other user of English – and not forgetting the students themselves.

This approach gives us all the chance to make our exploration of grammar immediately applicable to our own situations. If we know the set of circumstances in which passive constructions are used, the argument goes, we're in a better position to judge whether it would be appropriate for us to use a passive ourselves in our own speaking and writing, and better able to judge the effect of its use when we encounter it in our listening and reading. There's a confidence and satisfaction that comes from knowing we are in control over the choices that grammar makes available to us. When speaking and writing, we're confident we've chosen a construction that conveys the meaning and effect that we had in mind. When listening and reading, we're confident that we've appreciated the meaning and effect of the choices some other person had in mind.

The total set of choices that we make when using a language is called our *style*. The term is used in a variety of ways:

- the choices that make someone different from everyone else: 'my style', 'Shakespeare's style', 'Obama's style'.
- the choices that identify a relationship between user and audience: 'formal style', 'intimate style', 'official style'.
- the choices that identify membership of a group or organization: 'educated style', 'house style', 'the style of Metaphysical poetry'.
- the choices that identify membership of a profession: 'religious style', 'scientific style', 'journalese'.
- the choices that identify a genre: 'poetic style', 'prose style', 'email style'.

All aspects of language (vocabulary, orthography, pronunciation ...) contribute to the overall stylistic impression of a piece of speech or writing; but grammar has a special place. It provides the framework within which these aspects operate. It is the means whereby words, punctuation marks, tones of voice, and other features are integrated into a meaningful and effective whole. Grammar, in short, is the skeleton of style.

Style is a 'top-down' view of language use, a cumulative effect generated by all the choices a speaker/writer makes. It thus complements the 'bottom-up' way in which grammarians, prescriptive and descriptive, have typically approached the study of the subject. Both perspectives are essential. This is where the dictionary approach to grammar shows its limitations. Books such as Fowler's *Dictionary of Modern English Usage*, or a modern linguistic equivalent, such as Pam Peters' *The Cambridge Guide to English Usage*, provide illumination on points of detail, but leave it up to the reader to integrate usages into a stylistically coherent whole.

We need the two perspectives. Observing an individual point of grammar can indeed be illuminating, but at some stage we need to see how this point fits into spoken or written discourse. This involves making consistent choices in grammar as well as ensuring that these coincide with parallel choices in other areas of language. For example, a formal choice at one point in the discourse should be echoed by formal choices elsewhere. Contracted verb forms sit uncomfortably alongside *whom*:

I'd ask the gentleman to whom I've been talking.

And formal grammar sits uncomfortably alongside informal vocabulary:

I should ask the chap to whom I have been chatting.

Of course, it's always possible to break the stylistic norms to make an effect; but we have to know what the norms are before we can do this efficiently. As Robert Graves said, 'A poet has to master the rules of English grammar before he attempts to bend or break them.'

Mastering the rules – the authentic grammatical rules of the language, of course, not the unauthentic prescriptions of times past – is enlivened by the semantic/pragmatic approach, but it still requires attention to detail. Some hard work, in other words. Developing a satisfying spoken or written style doesn't come naturally. Children readily copy the style of the authors they read, the characters they see in films and television, and the writers they encounter on the Internet. Adult writers do the same, when they are starting out as authors. They all need to appreciate that, with rare exceptions, the style they admire is the result of considerable work on the part of the author, and that, if they want to develop their own stylistic individuality, they will need to work at it too.

These days it's much easier to explore the world of grammatical choices than it used to be. On a computer screen, we can make changes instantly, and press the 'undo' button if we don't like the result. It's now a routine experience to type a sentence onto a screen, and then alter its grammar – changing the clause types or the word order, adding or deleting words here and there … Often, writers vacillate. Oscar Wilde comes to mind:

> I was working on the proof of one of my poems all the morning, and took out a comma. In the afternoon I put it back again.

Authors take grammatical pains to achieve an individual style, and we all need to appreciate this. Honing alternatives until they're right is the first step towards developing our own stylistic individuality.

The semantic/pragmatic approach is at the opposite extreme from the prescriptive tradition, which was dominated by rules that users were obliged to follow in order to avoid social criticism. In that climate, there was, literally, no choice. It is also a considerable advance on the early descriptive tradition in linguistics, which gave an accurate and comprehensive account of the alternatives in grammatical usage but paid little attention to the social and stylistic factors that conditioned them. In that climate, there was apparently too much choice – which gave rise to the criticism that, for linguists, 'anything goes'.

The new approach points the way towards a meeting of minds. It provides a balance between structure and use, acknowledging the feelings of those who say that 'something has been lost' when grammatical terms are not known, yet recognizing the arguments of those who say that 'something can be gained' by using those terms as a means to the end of appreciating the glamour of language in use. It acknowledges some of the tenets of prescriptivism, such as the centrality of clarity and precision, but points us in the direction of where in grammar such aims can actually be achieved. It acknowledges the importance of prescriptions in language teaching, as long as these reflect the realities of usage and take into account meaning and effect.

The concept of a semantically and pragmatically conditioned grammatical choice, which is at the heart of the approach, is a persuasive and powerful one. It has its parallels in other areas of language, such as vocabulary (when people talk about 'choosing the best word ...'). It is a central notion in the study of literature, where critics explain the choices that authors have made. It is at the heart of theatrical performance, when directors and actors make 'choices' in interpreting a character or a line. It is echoed in many a definition of personal style, such as Jonathan Swift's 'proper words in proper places'. And it underpins the professional appearance of all occupational varieties of language, whether spoken or written. We tend to overlook the role of grammar, when we encounter the outpourings of lawyers, priests, journalists, scientists, advertisers, and sports commentators – to name just half a dozen professions. Their vocabulary is usually a far more noticeable feature of their worlds; but they all need grammar in order to make sense, and the way they form their sentences can be just as distinctive.

19

Grammar on the job

Grammar forms an important part of the identity of any occupation that relies on the use of language. In some contexts, such as religious and legal English, the grammatical distinctiveness is so unusual that the variety could never be mistaken for anything else. Only one English style is characterized by the use of a vocative *O*, old second-person pronouns, and archaic verb forms, all seen in this prayer for rain from the sixteenth-century *Book of Common Prayer*, still used in Anglican churches today:

> O God, heavenly Father, who by thy Son Jesus Christ
> hast promised to all them that seek thy kingdom, and the
> righteousness thereof, all things necessary to their bodily
> sustenance: Send us, we beseech thee, in this our necessity,
> such moderate rain and showers, that we may receive
> the fruits of the earth to our comfort, and to thy honour;
> through Jesus Christ our Lord. Amen.

Religious English displays other distinctive grammatical features too, less likely to be noticed until contrasted with other styles. It's not normal, for instance, to address someone with a name followed by a relative clause:

> John, who gave me a lift to work this morning, can I talk
> to you for a moment?

but this is perfectly normal in a prayer of invocation.

In the same way, only one English style is characterized by page-long punctuationless sentences, including ceremonial phrasing and lists of alternatives, as in this extract from a statement of guarantee:

> ... no release settlement discharge or arrangement which may have been given or made on the faith of any such assurance security or payment shall prejudice or affect your right to recover from the undersigned to the full extent of this Guarantee as if such assurance security payment release settlement discharge or arrangement (as the case may be) had never been granted given or made ...

It's not difficult to see why such complex sentences have arisen. Legal statements have to be generally applicable yet sufficiently specific to apply to individual circumstances. The sentences are long because they integrate several issues in a single statement and try to anticipate all eventualities. The aim is to reduce the uncertainty about whether the law applies in a particular case. Over the years a formulation has been repeatedly tested, and when found lacking, has been added to – hence such lists as 'assurance, security, payment, release ...' Punctuation is avoided in these formulations because a case can be won or lost based on the implications surrounding the use of a mark such as a comma or semi-colon.

The result is a style that requires expertise to be understood. It's often criticized by those who demand 'plain English' in legal documents; and it's often parodied, as in Don Sandburg's *Legal Guide to Mother Goose* (1978). Here's the beginning of his accident report on Jack and Jill, who, as the nursery rhyme records 'Went up a hill / To fetch a pail of water...'

The party of the first part hereinafter known as Jack ... and
...
The party of the second part hereinafter known as Jill ...

Ascended or caused to be ascended an elevation of undetermined height and degree of slope, hereinafter referred to as 'hill'.

Whose purpose it was to obtain, attain, procure, secure, or otherwise, gain acquisition to, by any and/or all means available to them, a receptacle or container, hereinafter known as 'pail', suitable for the transport of a liquid whose chemical properties shall be limited to hydrogen and oxygen, the proportions of which shall not be less than or exceed two parts for the first mentioned element and one part for the latter. Such combination will hereinafter be called 'water'.

Not all occupational varieties are as grammatically distinctive as religious and legal English; but, whatever the occupation, the syntax and morphology will always be there. They provide the variety with its individual stylistic skeleton, relating ideas to each other, expressing the progression of thought, and sequencing any activities that occur in the situation. The need to reflect events in the real world is not a feature of the above examples, but in some varieties, such as sports commentary, it's the governing factor.

Sports commentary

Radio sports commentators have an obvious job-defining task: to describe what is happening while it is happening – what has been called a 'play-by-play' commentary. They have to do other things too, of course, such as saying something relevant when no action is taking place – a 'colour-adding' commentary – but it's the play-by-play situation that has given the genre its distinctive grammatical character.

Commentary is dependent on the present tense for its success. It's an obvious point, but its frequency in commentaries is enough to distinguish this variety grammatically from any other:

> And it's Herrera with a lovely little pass to Rooney ...
> The blue is just waiting for the middle pocket ...
> It's a hanging curve ball ...
> Anderson comes in and bowls to ...
> And now Murray's serving for the match ...

The vocabulary – including the personal names – is what differentiates the various sports (respectively soccer, snooker, baseball, cricket, tennis), but it is the grammar that shows they have a common function.

If we follow through any one of these examples, we will see other features of sports commentary, especially its elliptical and repetitive character:

> ... Rooney back to Herrera ... Herrera to Lingard ...
> Lingard to Rooney ... Herrera again ...

The ellipsis is a reflection of the pace of the action. When a game is being played at speed, any reduction in the length of a sentence is a plus.

The word order is influenced by the way events unfold. We hear adverbials at the front of sentences when we would normally expect to hear them at the end:

> Over at second base is Castro – at third base is – Bird ...

The grammar seems to follow the commentator's eyes moving around the field. The pause after the verb is typical, as it can take a moment to establish who a player is. And this kind of uncertainty is reflected in the use of the passive construction (Chapter 17), which turns up in sports commentary more often than we might expect, especially in fast-moving games where there are a number of players. The reason is that commentators see a move before being able to determine the target of the move, so they need a construction in which they can say that something is happening without having to say who is making it happen. The passive is their lifesaver. Instead of 'Brown blocks Smith's shot at goal' we hear 'Smith's shot is blocked by – Brown.'

If the pace of a game slows, grammar can come to the commentator's aid again, by offering space for modifying words and phrases to help fill the time. Extra adjectives can be a godsend, and longer phrases and clauses coming after a noun even more so:

> ... Rooney sends a neat, cheeky, almost leisurely flick towards the goal ...
> ... and the ball lands in the safe hands of Federici, who's got Reading out of trouble more than once in this match ...

As always, when describing a style, we need to notice what is *not* there as well as what is. We won't hear the complicated subordinate clauses of a legal document, for instance. And if the commentator is fluent – as we would hope – there won't be any hedging expressions or hesitancies, such as *I mean, you know*, and *errrm*.

Breaking the rules

In occupational varieties such as religion, law, and sports commentary, the situational constraints are tight and well respected by practitioners. It would be virtually impossible for the professionals involved to use a kind of language that didn't conform to the expected norms. Indeed, in some circumstances, if the wrong kind of language was used, there might be social sanctions, such as (in law) a charge of contempt of court or (in religion) an accusation of blasphemy or heresy. However, not all occupations have their language so tightly constrained. In commercial advertising and journalism, there are grammatical rules that are generally followed, but the bending and breaking of those rules (p. 146) is commonplace and privileged.

Take the most basic rule of all: that writing intended for national public consumption should display present-day standard English grammar. This means an avoidance of nonstandard items such as *ain't*, regional dialect constructions such as *we was* or *I were sat*, and obsolete forms such as *ye* and *goeth*. But it doesn't take long before we see all these usages in print and online, often as eye-catching headlines for articles on web pages.

> 'We wuz robbed, viewers' – an article in *Daily Mail Online*
> 'There's gold in them there hills' – report in the *Telegraph* of a Scottish estate which contains untapped gold reserves
> 'The corporate taxman cometh' – article in the *Economist* on taxation
> 'Abandon sleep all ye that enter here' – report in *Trip Advisor*
> 'Nigeria ain't broke, it just needs to fix its tax system' – article in the *Guardian*

Community memory holds a large store of archaic or regional forms upon which headline writers and journalists frequently rely, usually to produce a catchy headline or to add an element of humour or parody to an article. And it doesn't take long before clever writers begin to play with the forms, taking them to new rhetorical heights. The idiomatic expression underlying the last example above – 'If it ain't broke, don't fix it' – has generated many variants:

> 'If it ain't broke, break it' – an article about writing new kinds of crime novels
> 'Hey, Twitter: if it ain't broke, don't add 9.8K characters to it' – a post about a Twitter proposal to allow longer tweets
> 'If it ain't broke, don't upgrade it' – a post on a new release of Photoshop
> 'If we can't fix it, it ain't broke' – a sign outside a car repair shop in the USA

An Internet search will bring to light many more.

Any grammatical rule can be bent or broken in the advertising world. For example, there's no theoretical upper limit to the number of adjectives we can have before a noun, but it's unusual to encounter more than two or three. Certainly not twelve, as in this ad from a few years ago:

> Why do you think we make Nuttall's Mintoes such a devilishly smooth cool creamy minty chewy round slow velvety fresh clean solid buttery taste?

Or again, we all have a free hand to make compound adjectives in a noun phrase, such as *best-selling* and *far-reaching*. But none of us outside advertising would go in for such coinages as *farmhouse-fresh* [taste], *rain-and-stain-resisting* [cloth], and *all-round-the-garden* [fertilizer]. A single instance might not be very noteworthy; but the repeated use of a grammatical feature becomes very noticeable in a longer ad. Note the number of pre-noun sequences (in bold) in this example from Geoffrey Leech's classic *English in Advertising* (1966):

> **Fantastic** acceleration from **the 95 bhp Coventry Climax OHC** engine, **more stopping** power from **the new 4-wheel servo-assisted disc** brakes and **greater** flexibility from **the all synchromesh close ratio** gearbox. **These and many other new** refinements combine to present **the finest and fastest light GT** car in the world.

There aren't many words left!

When we see written ads, our eyes are inevitably drawn to the visual features – the product image, the graphic design, the colours, the dramatic vocabulary. With spoken ads, our ears immediately pick up the rhythm and melody of the words (the 'jingles'), the repeated use of sounds ('Built better by Bloggs!'), and any melodramatic tones of voice. In neither case do we notice the role of grammar in making the words cohere, and yet it is critical. If we want to explain the effect of an ad, a newspaper article, a prayer – any distinctive use of language – then we have to pay careful attention to the grammatical features that give these styles their structure and coherence.

Explanations are what matter. It's never enough to simply describe the features of a style. We also need to ask *why* these features have developed in the way they have. In the case of law and religion, we have to go back into history to see the reasons – to do with case-law precedents and biblical sources. In the case of sports commentary we look to the ongoing action to explain the style. With ads, we have to enter the minds of the sales and marketing teams, whose aims are fourfold: to get us

– to notice the ad
– to maintain our interest so that we want to read it or listen to it
– to remember the name of the product

– and then, of course, to buy it.

Accordingly, a more judicious grammatical approach can be of benefit, in that it can help us think critically about the subtly persuasive ways in which advertising language operates. Something works 'better'? That's an unspecified comparative. Better than what? When? Where? This is economic linguistics. Grammar can save us money.

20

Explanations

'Explanations are what make grammar interesting for every-one,' I asserted in Chapter 18. 'Why?' is the question I hear most often from children having to learn about it and teach-ers having to teach it. It's asked whenever someone is praised for using grammar well or condemned for using it badly. It surfaces whenever people notice that they differ in their use of grammar, either in speaking or writing. And it especially comes to the fore when the subject forces itself on their atten-tion. Grammar can become intrusive, such as when unfamil-iar sentence patterns are encountered in government forms and legal documents (and organizations such as the Plain English Campaign present the texts in simpler syntax). It can become impressive when powerful sentences are encoun-tered in a great piece of oratory or a fine piece of writing (and aspiring public speakers and writers try to emulate them). In all these settings there comes a point when people ask themselves why grammar is the way it is, and wonder where all the rules and exceptions have come from.

We encounter new grammatical experiences in all kinds of everyday ways, such as when reading novels, listening to eloquent speakers, watching the plays put on by an amateur dramatic society, or encountering new grammatical styles on the Internet. The old prescriptive grammarians realized this, which is why they included sentences written by the best authors as examples of usage in their textbooks (p. 93).

The problem was that these were often so complex that they obscured the grammatical explanations they were intended to illustrate. In an introduction to grammar, authors should use the simplest sentences possible. But at a more advanced level a great deal of enjoyment and insight can be gained by exploring the grammatical craft of great writers.

Enjoyment and grammar? Many people cannot conceive that these two words could ever sit comfortably and positively together in one sentence. A recurrent theme of this book is that the negative associations that surround grammar are the result of unhappy learning experiences, in which complex sentences, artificial examples, pedantic rules, mechanical analyses, and poor explanations have combined to produce a penitential mindset: 'Grammar is good for me, and if it causes me mental anguish, then so be it'. In such a state of mind, grammar is as far away from glamour as it is possible to imagine.

How can such a mindset be changed? By showing that grammar is full of topics that are intriguing and inviting. I don't just mean to grammarians. I mean to anyone. People, I find, are fascinated when they realize just what it is they have acquired as a result of learning the grammar of their language – that they have mastered rules they never knew they knew. I've never met anyone who doesn't find it interesting to learn about the way little children like Suzie acquire grammar.

It all comes down to finding good examples that capture the imagination and instil a curiosity to discover how these rules work. That's when grammar moves in the direction of glamour. Here's an example that I find especially thought-provoking. It's a question I've often been asked, especially by people learning English as a foreign language. The explanation provides some answers but leaves some further questions. For a linguist, that's the best bit: new research horizons suddenly open up.

An example: binomials

For and against, ups and downs, out and about, by and large ...
Why do we say them this way? Nobody ever says *against and for, downs and ups, about and out, large and by*. We could call them idioms, but that's just a label, not an explanation. For why did the idioms come out that way and not the other way round? Not all strings of this kind are idioms anyway. We normally say *food and drink* and *time and effort*, but it would be perfectly possible to say *drink and food* or *effort and time*. So what is it that makes us opt for the first order and not the second, most of the time?

It's a topic that has attracted quite a lot of research. As always, grammarians have provided a technical term to describe what we're talking about. These strings are called *binomials*, from the Latin 'two names': each string consists of a pair of words belonging to the same word class and linked by a conjunction. *And* is the commonest conjunction, but *or* and *but* are also found (*sooner or later, strange but true*) and occasionally prepositions make a binomial (*rags to riches, little by little*). When the two parts can change their order, as in *effort and time*, the binomial is called *reversible*. When the two parts are frozen, as in *for and against*, the binomial is called *irreversible*. What is it that makes these phrases irreversible, or makes us prefer one sequence rather than the other? There isn't a simple answer: several factors are involved.

One of the obvious factors is length: the longer item comes second. This certainly seems to be the case with all the binomials in my first paragraph: in each case the second item has more sounds in it – more consonants or syllables. This explanation would tie in nicely with the way English follows the principle of end-weight that I discussed in Chapter 13. And a large number of binomials do follow the rule: *salt and vinegar, law and order, trials and tribulations, rest and relaxation, head and shoulders, bells and whistles, rich and famous, terms and conditions, out and about* ... So do *rank and file, black and white, heads or tails, long and short,* and *win or lose,* where the vowel in the first item is short and in the second is long. And so do *aches and pains, coal and steel,* and *short and sweet,* where the vowels are long in each case, but there are more consonants in the second item.

However, length won't explain why we say *wine and dine* or *rise and shine,* where the number of spoken consonants and vowels is the same in each word, and the length of the vowels is the same. There are cases, too, where the longer item comes first, as in *needle and thread* and *strange but true.* In others, the difference in length is so slight or variable that it would seem to have no effect, as in *back and forth* or *loud and clear,* where the order stays the same regardless of whether the speaker adds an extra consonant by pronouncing the *r* after the vowel.

Perhaps, then, the order is governed by the meaning of the words? Indeed, quite a large number of binomials can be explained on semantic grounds. Sometimes the first item comes chronologically before the second or causes the second: *born and bred, hand to mouth, life and death, rise and shine, kiss and make up, hit and run, smash and grab, old and grey.* Or the first word is perceived to be more powerful in society or more in control than the second: *men and women, man and wife, mother and child, father and son, cat and mouse.* Another trend is that the first item is perceived to have more positive connotations than the second: *cops and robbers, saints and sinners, heaven and hell, win or lose, strengths and weaknesses, soap and water, yes or no.* In cases like *head and shoulders, high and low, hill and dale, leaps and bounds, ups and downs, above and beyond, rise and fall,* and *an arm and a leg,* the critical point seems to be that the first item is 'above' the second. In cases like *tooth and nail, cloak and dagger,* and *fish and chips,* the first item seems to be more functionally distinctive: teeth cause more damage than nails, cloaks hide daggers, and we can have chips 'with everything'.

However, semantic thinking won't explain many other cases. What is going on with *bread and butter, milk and honey,* and *time and energy?* Here the two items seem to be equal in importance: is time more important or distinctive than energy? There seems to be more to it than simple length: a rhythmical factor is present. Compare the way the stressed (underlined) and unstressed syllables work in these cases:

bread and butter butter and bread
milk and honey honey and milk
time and energy energy and time

In the first column, there is just a single unstressed syllable between the two strong ones: this makes the rhythm conform to the basic 'tum-te-tum' or *stress-timed* rhythm of English – the kind of rhythm we hear in classical poetry ('The curfew tolls the knell of parting day'). In the second column, the rhythm is more disjointed, with two or three unstressed syllables separating the two strong ones. It seems that binomials like to conform to a regular rhythm.

That will explain several more binomials, but still not all. What's happening with monosyllabic pairs, such as *knife and fork, nuts and bolts, deaf and dumb, black and white, beck and call?* Length isn't a factor now; nor is rhythm or meaning. It would be difficult to argue that *black* is more important than *white* or *nuts* more important than *bolts.* To explain these we need to consider other factors.

In quite a few cases, it seems that we like to put first words where the vowels are articulated higher up in the mouth or further towards the front of the mouth. With *deaf and dumb*, the vowel in *deaf* is front, whereas the vowel in *dumb* is further back. Similarly, the vowel in *knife* is front and high; the vowel in *fork* is back and low. Other examples include *this or that, cats and dogs, spick and span, ifs and buts, tit for tat,* [when all's] *said and done.*

These factors all work independently of each other and reinforce each other. So a binomial in which one item was shorter, semantically more important, contributed to a regular stress pattern, and had a front vowel would definitely put that item first! And in many cases we see the way combinations of these factors reinforce each other: *black and blue* shows a front and short vowel in *black* and a long and back vowel in *blue.* And the same kind of combination drives *back and forth, beck and call, flesh and bones, fast and loose, nuts and bolts, wind and rain, give and take, big and small.*

Of all the factors, the semantic ones seem to be the most influential, and the rhythmical ones the next most important. But there are binomials that seem to break most or all of the rules. Why is it *eyes and ears* and not *ears and eyes?* Why *chalk and cheese* and not *cheese and chalk?* Why *huff and puff?* Why *man and boy?* Why have *ladies and gentlemen, bride and groom,* and *mum and dad* (*mom and pop*) predominated, given the traditional direction of *man and wife, his and hers, boys and girls, brother and sister,* and so on?

In some cases we can find a historical reason – perhaps a quotation that influenced subsequent usage. For example, we can trace *in sickness and in health* back to the wedding ceremony in *The Book of Common Prayer.* But why did the translators go for that order, rather than *in health and in sickness?* The chosen version breaks most of the rules: the first item is longer, it is negative, and it causes three unstressed syllables to come together. Was it simply that the high vowel of *sickness* took precedence over the lower vowel of *health*? Were they attracted by the rhythm of the phrase as a whole? Whatever the reason in the sixteenth century, the order has become increasingly fixed over the years. Frequently used reversible binomials tend to become irreversible in time.

From a literary point of view, irreversible binomials are a gift, as authors can go out of their way to reverse them in order to create an effect. So, an online history lesson about the way wartime Leipzig was taken by the Americans and later ceded to the Russians was headed 'A Matter of Take and Give'. And a long-running TV sitcom was called 'The Fall and Rise of Reginald Perrin'. It's a simple but effective way of drawing attention to a topic. An article about an inarticulate government's failure to respond to something? 'Dumb and deaf'. A restaurant review? 'Dine and wine'. An economic downturn? 'Riches to rags'.

As always, with a grammatical enquiry, we are left with some loose ends that the analysis cannot explain. That is why so many research papers end with a statement that 'further research is needed'. It is in the academic journals that we see the story of English grammar continuing to be told. And there are always two sides to the story, two kinds of explanation: one looks back into history; the other looks around the world of the present day.

21
Grammatical change – now

Living languages always change. The changes reflect new social situations, inventions, fashions, contacts, personalities, attitudes, opinions – anything, in short, that makes us different today from what we were yesterday. Some people do not like it; some go out of their way to try to prevent it; but their task is hopeless. The only languages that don't change are dead ones. And English, with its remarkable global spread and extensive Internet presence, changes more often than most.

Dr Johnson appreciated the inevitability of language change when he reflected, in the Preface to his *Dictionary*, that those who want to fix a language are trying to do something 'which neither reason nor experience can justify'. They are trying 'to lash the wind'. It is a crucial perspective that needs to be explained – not least to children, who would otherwise find the existence of usage alternatives confusing and (in an exam setting) alarming. Teachers play an important role here, drawing attention in class to the normality of language change, and the kinds of variation that result from it – for changes affect different parts of society in different ways and at different rates. A grammatical change that affects American English might take place earlier and more rapidly than in British English – or vice versa. A change may appear in speech but not in writing, in informal writing but not in formal writing, among young people before old, among women before men, and so on. We all need to understand the reasons for the changes, to explore the different social situations in which they occur, to develop a feeling for different stylistic effects, and – these days, for children and parents – to see why one usage rather than another will get good marks in the latest national grammar test.

Vocabulary is the most noticeable sign of language change: the latest words make headlines each year when they're included in a dictionary for the first time. A new word can enter the language overnight, if the media make something of it. On 4 October 1957, few in the English-speaking world would ever have heard the word *sputnik*; on 5 October, everyone had. Changes in grammar don't make the headlines, nor do they enter the language overnight – or even over-year. Over-decades and over-centuries, rather. But in the long run they are more pervasive than vocabulary. The grammatical changes that were taking place imperceptibly in 1957 are a regular part of the language now, affecting everyone and frequently encountered, while *sputnik* is history.

One of these slowly moving changes is the steady increase in the use of the progressive form of verbs (*stative* verbs – see Chapter 8), especially in the present tense, and especially in speech: *We're having to address the issues* (instead of the simple form, *We have to address the issues*), *You're living in London now?* (instead of, *You live in London now?*). When a firm like McDonald's begins to do this in a slogan, it's clear that the trend in usage is firmly established: 'I'm lovin' it.' A generation ago, it would have been 'I love it.' And now I see the progressive everywhere. My morning cereal packet asks me 'Feeling creative?', not 'Feel creative?'

How are we knowing that this is a general change, and not just a minor stylistic idiosyncrasy? We might register the development intuitively, but none of us would have the breadth of linguistic experience to be able to say confidently that it was affecting the language as a whole. We need to look at lots of verbs that previously would not have used the progressive form, and check that the same developments are taking place in American, British, and other major regional varieties of English, in writing as well as in speech, and across many genres. This is where *corpus studies* come into their own.

Keyword: corpus

A corpus is a large collection of spoken or written texts representing a particular time, place, or genre (such as fiction, academic prose, newspapers, legal documents, conversation, letters). The largest corpora consist of hundreds of millions of words, and such sizes are needed in order to bring to light trends such as the one just described. Some fairly small corpora have been available since the 1960s, but the largest ones had to await the arrival of computers and the development of large storage and fast search and retrieval facilities. It's an exciting field of research, as it's still in its early days, and many areas of the language, past and present, have had little or no investigation.

So, let's take further the trend just described. Which stative verbs would *not* have used the progressive form fifty years ago? The corpus studies show that most of the time people would have said things like this:

I want a new fridge.
I intend to apply for a new job.
I need a new coat.
It concerns me a lot.
It matters to me greatly.

I think I should go.
I know the answer.

This is familiar usage. Today, we're increasingly hearing (we increasingly hear?) the following:

I'm wanting a new fridge.
I'm intending to apply for a new job.
I'm needing a new coat.
It's concerning me a lot.
It's mattering to me greatly.
I'm thinking I should go.

It's a trend that's happening right now, so not every reader of this book will react in the same way. Some will feel comfortable with *wanting*, for example, and uncomfortable with *needing*; some will have the opposite feeling; some will use both; some will use neither. You may have noticed that I left off my list the final example: *I'm knowing the answer*. This is because *know* is one of the verbs that seems to have been most resistant to the change. There are very few instances of it so far in the corpus studies. But the number is growing. In some parts of the world, such as India, it's well established. I think it'll become perfectly normal British and American English over the next twenty years.

The process takes time. The first step is when we hear *knowing* in the speech of others and read it in their writing. To begin with, it might jar. But after a while we might not even notice it, even though we would never use it ourselves. Then, gradually, as it becomes widespread, we find ourselves using it. You can test yourself on the point now. Did you notice my use of *knowing* in the first line of the last paragraph before the sub-heading above?

An even more subtle trend is in the use of the auxiliary

verb *must*. It's a verb that has various meanings, such as obligation. If I say you *must* do something, I mean that in my view you're obliged to do it.

> You must leave immediately.

When I use it, I'm asserting my authority over you. So this is the kind of usage that sits comfortably in a society dominated by hierarchical social relationships and a strong sense of social decorum, where one class of person tells another what they 'must' do. In short: it is a prescriptive word.

It was, accordingly, very frequent in the eighteenth and nineteenth centuries, and has steadily become less used as society has changed. It has been replaced by other verbs that soften the force of the obligation, such as *got to* (*gotta*) and *have to* (*hafta*), which have all been greatly increasing in frequency over the past century.

> You have to leave immediately.
> You've got to leave immediately.
> You ought to leave immediately.
> You'd better leave immediately.

Any of these carries a more personal, more advisory, more friendly tone. There may even be a hint of apology.

The same change has been happening to other uses of *must*. For instance, I'm totally convinced about your behaviour if I declare:

> I must say you're doing the wrong thing.

This is a different use of the verb. There's no sense of obligation here: I'm not forcing myself to say you're wrong. Rather, I'm choosing to say it, with the *must* suggesting that in my mind I'm not going to tolerate any disagreement. However, something different is conveyed if I express myself this way:

I have to say you're doing the wrong thing.

Now there's a hint of reluctance. I've reduced the strength of my commitment.

Put these two uses together and we can feel a social and psychological change taking place towards equality and seeing the other person's point of view. It is a less ego-centred view of the world. We might expect to see such a change in any English-speaking society that is becoming more egalitarian: for example, in the USA there was a sharp decrease in *must* and an increase in *have to* (and others) around the time of the American Civil War. But whatever the explanation, the statistical facts are clear. In one big study, using the Diachronic Corpus of Present-Day Spoken English, between 1960 and 1990 the use of *must* reduced by 51 per cent. We simply don't use it so much any more.

These changes are slow-moving, and that is as it should be. Grammar is the means through which we make sense to each other (p. xvi), and if it changed too quickly, this would not be possible. So we don't expect to see much grammatical difference between parent and child; but the further back in time we go, the more such differences are going to emerge. Go back a couple of grandfathers, and we start to notice ways of using grammar that today are impossible. Go back ten grandfathers and the contrast is dramatic. And what if we go back twenty or so grandfathers, to the beginning of Anglo-Saxon times?

Interlude: Pluralsy

Grammatical changes regularly attract the interest of satirists. *Punch* magazine fired off several shots in its issue of 19 March 1924 (p. 290). Evidently, The Society for Pure English had recently recommended a sparing use of foreign plurals.

Though we do not recommend a
Change of plural for 'agenda'.
And we always understand a
Careful list of 'memoranda';
Though we can't eliminate a
Careless publisher's 'errata',
May the man who says 'gymnasia'
Be afflicted with aphasia!
If we do not check this mania
We shall cultivate 'gerania',
For the gardener, though he delves,
Knows more Latin than ourselves.
We shall see him planting 'gea'
In the gardens of 'musea',
Also 'scillae' in the 'loci'
Of 'narcissi' and of 'croci'.
We shall talk of 'animalia';
Our relations from Australia,
On arriving at Victoria,
Will encumber our 'emporia'
Buying 'camerae' as well as
Silk 'umbrellae,' not umbrellas.
Now, if this is not abated,
With the quite uneducated
Every 'us' will turn to 'i',
'Omnibus' to 'omnibi'.
Each one of the lot of us is
Fond of hippopotamuses,

And some of us at least
Feel the Gateway of the East
Will be creaking on its hinges
If our sphinxes turn to 'sphinges'.
If we do not cut our losses
And retain 'rhinoceroses',
We shall find the Hellespont is
Full of Greek 'rhinocerontes'
All trying hard to swim it;
And there won't be any limit
To the Latin, Greek and Bulgar
Of a tongue that once was vulgar,
When the English of our mothers
Is the property of others.

22

Grammatical change – then

How much grammatical change has there been since English began? The general impression, from reading Old English, represented in manuscripts from the seventh to the eleventh century AD, is that there has been a huge amount. But the differences shouldn't blind us to the continuities. Old English often gives new readers the impression that it is a foreign language, but this is partly a result of the unfamiliar features of the alphabet and partly because so much of the vocabulary has died out. When we ignore these factors, and look at the grammar, the syntactic continuity with the present day is notable.

Old English

Here's a sentence from a conversation piece about occupations composed by Abbot Ælfric around the year 1000. (The þ letter represents the sound of *th*; the æ letter represents the sound *a* as in *cat*.)

> *Ic eom geanwyrde monuc, ond sincge ælce dæg seofon tida mid gebroþrum.*
> I am professed monk, and sing each day seven times with brothers.

The word-for-word translation highlights some differences in the way we now use the articles *a* and *the*, and the word-endings are unfamiliar, but the word order leaves us in no doubt that grammatically this is the same language as the one we use today.

Here's a longer passage. It's from a letter written by King Alfred the Great in the early 890s to Bishop Wærferþ of Worcester, contrasting the early days of Christianity in England with his own time, following the destruction caused by the Vikings, and complaining about the loss of learning. Again, I'll give a word-for-word translation. (The ð letter was another way of representing the sound of *th*; the ʒ letter represented a soft (fricative) form of *g*.)

swa clæne heo wæs oþfeallenu on Angel-cynne
so completely it was fallen-off in England

þæt swiðe feawa wæron beheonan Humbre
that very few were this-side Humber

þe hira þeʒnunga cuðen understandan on Englisc
who their service-books could understand in English

oþþe furðum an ærendʒewrit of Lædene on Englisc areccan,
or even one written-message from Latin into English translate,

and ic wene þætte naht maniʒe beʒeondan Humbre næren.
and I think that not many beyond Humber weren't.

There are more differences coming to light now, but the language is unmistakeably English, with clear signs of its Germanic origin – still seen in modern German – in the verbs sometimes placed at the end of clauses.

It's important to look at prose first, when evaluating major trends in grammatical change. If we look only at poetry, the constraints of having to write in lines with a particular length and rhythm can have a marked effect on word order, making a state of the language seem more different from the present day than it actually was. It's the same today. Imagine what a grammatical description would look like, in a thousand years time, if someone were to describe present-day English on the basis of examples like these:

> Sleepless, by the windowpane I stare (Dannie Abse)
> In the burrows of the Nightmare / Where Justice naked is (W. H. Auden)
> anyone lived in a pretty how town / (with up so floating many bells down) (E. E. Cummings)

These lines show what can be done creatively with grammar – how the normal rules can be bent and broken (p. 146) in the service of poetry – but they wouldn't provide a reliable guide to what those norms are.

So, if we time-travelled back to Anglo-Saxon England, speaking modern English, and met Beowulf, speaking Old English prose, would we understand each other? We'd each have trouble with the vocabulary. He would need a dictionary to look up our modern French- and Latin-derived words; we would need one to look up his long-since-lost Germanic ones. We'd also need to get used to each other's accents. But we'd both recognize most of the important grammatical words that build our sentences. They haven't changed much – sometimes, not at all. The Alfred extract shows some of them – *wæs, and, on, of, þæt* – and other parts of that text show further identities that we would immediately understand, such as *me, we, to,* and *is*. We'd have to get used to our different pronunciations of such words as *naht* 'not', *ic* 'I', *eow* 'you', and *hu* 'how'. And Beowulf would wonder what had happened to some of his word-endings, such as *wæron* 'were', and beginnings, such as *næren*, where the 'were' has a negative *n-* prefix, thus meaning 'weren't'. But we would both feel at home with the basic structure of our respective sentences.

The problem would be greater for us than for Beowulf. Inflections (p. 33) were an important part of Old English grammar, and these hardly appear in modern English. Beowulf would notice their absence, but the word order of a modern English sentence would be enough to enable him to grasp what was being said. It wouldn't be so easy for us. If we failed to pay attention to his word-endings, we would sometimes misunderstand what he was saying. If he wanted to tell us that 'the lady saw the man', he could rely on the endings to say who was doing what to whom, and he wouldn't have to bother about the order of the words. So that sentence might be expressed with a modern English order:

seo hlæfdige seah þone guman

Or, in principle (for not all word orders are equally well represented in the surviving manuscripts), with the order changed:

þone guman seah seo hlæfdige
seah þone guman seo hlæfdige
seah seo hlæfdige þone guman

They all mean the same thing. In each case, we know 'who is doing what to whom' because the endings tell us. In traditional terms (Chapter 5), *seo* and the absence of an ending on *hlæfdige* show that 'lady' is in the nominative case; *þone* and the ending on *guman* show that 'man' is in the accusative case. And this is confirmed when we see the sentence 'the man saw the lady'. This would be:

se guma seah þa hlæfdigan

The endings have changed. Now *guma* is nominative and *hlæf-dige* accusative.

It wouldn't take long for our ears to tune in to the importance of these endings. But even if we failed to notice them, or the corresponding ones on adjectives and verbs, we'd probably find ourselves getting the gist of what was being said. And if we tried to speak Old English ourselves, without the correct endings, Beowulf would usually understand us. I regularly get my word-endings wrong when speaking a language like German, that I don't know very well. I get some strange looks, but on the whole people grasp what I'm trying to say.

Middle English

If we continued on our time-travelling way, moving back towards the present day, we would find that the inflectional issue wouldn't cause us a problem for much longer. By the end of the Anglo-Saxon period, most of the endings were slowly disappearing, and word order was becoming the main signal of grammatical relationships, as it is today. If we called in on Chaucer, around the year 1400, and listened in to how he was teaching his son some science, this is what we would hear him saying:

> Lyte Lowys my sone, I aperceyve wel by certeyne evydences thyn abilite to lerne sciences touching nombres and proporciouns; and as wel considre I thy besy praier in special to lerne the tretys of the Astrelabie.

It's the opening sentence (in the edition by F. N. Robinson) of his *Treatise on the Astrolabe* – an astronomical computing device. Does it need translating? Not from a grammatical point of view. Several of the spellings are unfamiliar, showing the influence of French, and some of the words have meanings a little different from today, but if we replace these by modern forms we get something that is very close to what we would say today:

> Little Lewis my son, I perceive well by certain evidences thine ability to learn sciences touching numbers and proportions; and as well consider I thy busy [anxious] prayer in special to learn the treatise of the Astrolabe.

The differences are obvious, and minor. *Evidence* isn't used with a plural ending in standard English any more (though it's resurfacing in the speech of many second-language learners of English). We wouldn't any longer say *consider I*. Today we'd say *specially* or *especially* for *in special*. *Thy* and *thine* would both be replaced by *your*. And that's it.

A few more distinctive features of Middle English grammar emerge as we broaden our search. In the verb, for instance, we still find some endings that would later be lost. Take the verb *sing*. The first person form ('I sing') was *singe*, the second ('thou') was *singes* or *singest*; the third ('he, she, it') was *singes* or *singeth*. The variations reflected different regional usage. The *-s* ending of the third person, for instance, was widespread in the north of England, and only later spread south to become the standard use today. And then, as now, there were many irregular verbs, such as *halp* ('helped'), whose forms differed from those in modern English. The biggest problem in reading Middle English is the way a word appears in so many different spellings, partly reflecting regional variations in pronunciation, partly individual scribal practices. What appears as *help* in one place might be *halp*, *healp*, *heolp*, or *elp* in others.

Middle English grammar hasn't entirely disappeared. Christmas carollers use an old verb ending without a second thought when they sing 'Ding dong merrily on high':

> E'en so here below, below,
> Let steeple bells be swungen,
> And 'Io, io, io!'
> By priest and people sungen.

And the *-th* ending appears still in 'Thirty days hath September', the title of Eugene O'Neill's play *The Iceman Cometh* (1939), and many a quirky newspaper headline or TV show. 'The Taxman Cometh' headed an episode of the series *Law and Order* in 2010.

Early Modern English

If Middle English is grammatically very familiar to modern eyes, Early Modern English is even more so. We're now talking about a 300-year period from the middle of the fifteenth century. It's usually taken to begin around the time of the arrival of printing in Britain (1476) and to end around the lifetime of Dr Johnson (died 1784). Right in the middle of the period we encounter Shakespeare. Would our time traveller have been able to follow his grammar without any problems?

For the most part. We can read page after page of Shakespearean prose and not notice any difference. The poetry is a different matter, as it always is, because the need to fit a sentence into a metrical line can cause all sorts of unusual variations in word order. Mercutio in *Romeo and Juliet* (1.4.70) tells us about the fairy queen Mab, who comes at night and makes people dream their desires. Note the metrically induced syntactic changes as she gallops

> O'er ladies' lips, who <u>straight on kisses dream</u>,
> Which oft the angry Mab <u>with blisters plagues</u>,
> Because their breaths with sweetmeats <u>tainted are</u>.

Word-endings too can vary depending on the rhythm of the line. When the Duchess of Gloucester complains about one of her political enemies in *Henry VI Part 2* (2.4.52), we see the old and modern third-person endings side by side, because the *-eth* adds a syllable that meets the demand of the metre:

> For Suffolk, he that can do all in all
> With her that hateth thee and hates us all

It's a nice regular iambic pentameter, thanks to the availability of the two endings. But the *-eth* was already dying out in Shakespeare's day, and a century later wouldn't be seen at all, other than in writers being deliberately archaic – or, as with *the taxman cometh*, being jocular.

Prose dialogue doesn't present such issues. Here's part of the dialogue between Prince Hal, Falstaff, and their confederates, when they are about to rob some travellers in *Henry IV Part 1* (2.2.58):

> PRINCE HAL: Sirs, you four shall front them in the narrow lane. Ned Poins and I will walk lower – if they scape from your encounter, then they light on us.
> PETO: How many be there of them?
> GADSHILL: Some eight or ten.
> FALSTAFF: Zounds, will they not rob us?
> PRINCE HAL: What, a coward, Sir John Paunch?
> FALSTAFF: Indeed, I am not John of Gaunt your grandfather, but yet no coward, Hal.
> PRINCE HAL: Well, we leave that to the proof.
> POINS: Sirrah Jack, thy horse stands behind the hedge. When thou needest him, there thou shalt find him. Farewell, and stand fast!

Once again, there are some vocabulary differences, such as *scape* for *escape*, and old words such as *sirrah* and *zounds*, but in grammar the only notable point of contrast with modern English is the use of *thou* and *thy*, and the associated forms *needest* and *shalt*. This is worth exploring further (see Interlude on p. 185), for there are nuances associated with the use of *thou*, as opposed to *you*, which add greatly to our appreciation of the relationship between characters. But if we fail to notice them, our comprehension of the dialogue isn't going to be affected. *Thou* is so often encountered in modern English, in religious settings, children's comics, and historical writing, as well as being widespread in regional dialects, that it is a familiar archaism.

The grammatical difficulties we find in Shakespeare are sporadic, and for the most part are points that we would consider nonstandard today, even though we understand what's being said perfectly well. For instance when Gonzalo says in *The Tempest* (3.3.20) 'My old bones aches', we notice the odd agreement between the subject and the verb. When in *A Midsummer Night's Dream* (2.2.132) Helena regrets that she 'nor never can' deserve a sweet look from Demetrius, we recall the disapproval of 'double negatives' in present-day standard English. When Mark Antony says 'That was the most unkindest cut of all' (*Julius Caesar*, 3.2.184) or Bottom says 'for the more better assurance' (*A Midsummer Night's Dream*, 4.1.18), we note the way that double comparatives and double superlatives were once used. Every now and again we come across an old form of a verb, such as *holp* (for *helped*), *digged* (for *dug*), and *writ* (for *wrote*), or an old plural, such as *musics, courages*, and *informations*, but none of these usages truly interfere with our comprehension.

Even the so-called 'ethical dative' construction rarely causes a problem. This is the way a personal pronoun can be used after a verb to express such notions as 'to' or 'for' (the old dative construction, p. 36). When Cardinal Pandulph in *King John* (3.4.146) tells the Dauphin that 'John lays you plots', he means 'John lays plots for you to fall into.' It's a construction hardly used today – though I remember it in the popular song 'Cry me a river', so it's not totally alien – but it can mislead us if we aren't prepared for it. However, we aren't alone. The usage was already dying out in Shakespeare's day, and any confusion we might have now was also possible then. In *The Taming of the Shrew* (1.2.5) we see its comic possibilities. Petruchio and his servant Grumio arrive at Hortensio's front door. Grumio is a typical clown, who gets his words wrong (*rebused* is a mistake for *abused*), and here he misunderstands his master's grammar too:

PETRUCHIO: Here, sirrah Grumio, knock, I say.
GRUMIO: Knock, sir? Whom should I knock? Is there any
man has rebused your worship?
PETRUCHIO: Villain, I say, knock me here soundly.
GRUMIO: Knock you here, sir? Why, sir, what am I, sir,
that I should knock you here, sir?
PETRUCHIO: Villain, I say, knock me at this gate,
And rap me well, or I'll knock your knave's pate.
GRUMIO: My master is grown quarrelsome. I should knock
you first,
And then I know after who comes by the worst.

Petruchio means by *Knock me here* 'Knock on the door for me'. Grumio interprets it as meaning 'Hit me here', as it would in modern English.

By Early Modern English, our sense of grammatical change has altered. We notice the points of difference, not because they interfere with our ability to understand what's being said, but because they contrast with what today is held to be acceptable, or 'correct', in standard modern English. Every now and then I see people commenting on Shakespeare's 'bad grammar' – usages like *nor never* – and it's important to point out that this is an unwarrantable imposition of modern values. Nobody would have thought *nor never* was 'wrong' in the sixteenth century. Queen Elizabeth would have used it. Here's an example, in her response to parliament in 1566:

> At this present it is not convenient, nor never shall be without some peril unto you, and certain danger unto me.

The condemnation came much later, when the prescriptive grammarians took against it, kings and queens notwithstanding, and succeeded in eliminating it from educated use.

So does this mean that, by the end of the eighteenth century, grammar had reached the state it's in today? Not entirely.

Interlude: Thou vs you

Languages regularly borrow from each other – usually in vocabulary, but sometimes in grammar. In the Middle Ages, after the Norman Conquest, the French-educated elite in Britain probably influenced the growth of the genitive *of* construction as an alternative to the '*s-*' construction, so that people began saying *the daughter of the queen* alongside *the queen's daughter* (compare French *la fille de la reine*). And when French nobility began to use the plural pronoun *vous* ('you') as a form of respect to one person instead of the singular pronoun *tu*, we see a similar shift in English taking place between *you*-forms (*you, your, yours, yourself, yourselves*) and *thou*-forms (*thou, thee, thy, thine, thyself*). As a result, a new stylistic contrast emerged.

In Shakespeare, we sense a shift in the temperature of a relationship when a character switches from *thou* to *you* or vice versa. Hamlet is maintaining an expected politeness between upper-class people when he tells Ophelia 'I loved you not.' A few seconds later, he destroys that rapport with 'Get thee to a nunnery.' Changing the pronoun always signals a change in attitude or a difference in relationship. We see *thee* becoming *you* in Act 4 Scene 1 of *Much Ado About Nothing*, when Benedick switches from being a lover to being a business-like soldier, having agreed to fight Claudio on Beatrice's behalf:

By this hand, I love thee. [line 321]
I will kiss your hand, and so I leave you. [line 326]

We see the opposite switch in *King Lear* Act 1 Scene 1, when Lear reacts angrily to Cordelia's replies, having previously spoken to her courteously:

What can you say? [line 84]
Thy truth then be thy dower. [line 107]

And when half-blind Old Gobbo, in Act 2 Scene 2 of *The Merchant of Venice*, realizes that the man he thinks to be a stranger is actually his son, we see the appropriate change:

> I cannot think you are my son. [line 81]
> Thou art mine own flesh and blood. [line 86]

23

Into living memory (almost)

On 5 September 1819 the poet John Keats sends an apologetic letter to his publisher John Taylor, in which he writes:

> Had I known of your illness I should not of written in such fierry phrase in my first Letter.

'Should not of written'? From such a great poet? It must have been just a slip, because later on in the same letter he writes 'You should not have delayed.' What interests me is to find this confusion 200 years ago. It isn't just a modern thing, as some critics say. That identity in pronunciation between the preposition *of* and the unstressed form of the auxiliary verb *have* has been around a long time.

Points like this are difficult to spot because there's a huge tendency to correct. The Gutenberg online text of Keats's letters, for example, silently changes his *of* to *have* in the above example. We have to go back to the original manuscripts to be sure we are reading exactly what an author wrote. The early nineteenth century was especially prone to editorial correcting, being very sensitive to the prescriptive rules that had not long before been formulated. As we saw in Chapter 12, it was a time when Lindley Murray's grammar ruled in the schools. So when we read Jane Austen, for example, we do not read what she wrote: we read what an editor in her publishing house, hypersensitive to the way society had begun to follow those rules, would like her to have written.

Two centuries ago

Examining the usage of a writer like Keats quickly shows how little grammatical change has taken place over the past 200 years. The vast majority of his writing is unremarkable, from this point of view. Take the beginning of his letter to Mrs Ann Wylie (6 August 1818). It could have been written today – ignoring idiosyncrasies of spelling and punctuation – apart from just four small points (italicized below):

> My dear Madam –
> It was a great regret to me that I should leave all my friends, just at the moment when I might have helped to soften away the time for them. I *wanted not* to leave my Brother Tom, but more especially, beleive me, I should like to have remained near you, were it but for an atom of consolation, after parting with so dear a daughter; My brother George *has ever been* more than a brother to me, he has been my greatest friend, & I can never forget the sacrifice you have made for his happiness. As I walk along the Mountains here, I am full of these things, & *lay* in wait, as it were, for the pleasure of seeing you, immediately on my return to town. I wish above all things, to say a word of Comfort to you, but I *know not* how.

The *not* following the verb is the most noticeable feature – something that can be seen in several of his letters from that time. The use of the adverb *ever* is less distinctive, but forms part of a pattern of adverb use no longer found, but seen elsewhere in Keats in *I am well disappointed* and *I was much disappointed*.

Keats's verb system is very close to that of modern English, but every now and then a usage appears which shows it is not identical (all the following examples are from 1818–20):

> I have been returned from Winchester this fortnight.
> No snuff being to be had in the village ...
> I wonder your brother don't put ...
> Now I will return to Fanny – it rains.

There are also occasional differences in the way noun phrases are formed:

> When none such troubles oppress me ...
> You see what a many words it requires ...
> I could not make out I had so many acquaintance ...

And there are some unexpected anticipations of usages which, like *should of*, are often said to be of modern origin. For example, in recent years we have increasingly heard people using an emphatic reflexive pronoun instead of a personal pronoun: instead of *They saw me*, we hear *They saw myself*. Those who hate this usage tend to say it's new. Keats shows it isn't:

> As far as they regard myself I can despise all events.

A century ago

My grandparents could have met children's writer E. Nesbit, who died in 1924; and their grandparents could have met Keats (who died in 1821). Certainly any child who was into reading during the first decade of the twentieth century would have fallen in love with *Five Children and It* (1902), *The Phoenix and the Carpet* (1904), with which I opened this book (p. xviii), and *The Railway Children* (1906). They are still widely read, so the features of English grammar that distance their language from the present day must still be part of modern linguistic intuitions, even though they are no longer heard. We see two on the opening page of *Five Children and It*. The children have just arrived at their country house:

> *Everyone* got *its* legs kicked or *its* feet trodden on in the
> scramble to get out of the carriage ...
> she [mother] *seemed to wish* to see the boxes carried in

It seems that the problem of how to refer to *everyone* with a pronoun was as awkward to handle then as it is still. And other usage issues lurk within examples taken from other century-old sources:

> Usedn't people to have no homes ...?
> Oh, please, mayn't we have another?

This one has definitely gone out of use:

> on account of me being going to make a respectable
> young man happy ...

But the following examples simply seem dated:

> But father said they might keep the egg.
> It's simply quite too dreadfully awful.

Is this use of *quite too* completely dead? It was already being satirized in the 1880s: a song written by Robert Coote to poke fun at the fashionable aestheticism of the time was called 'Quite too utterly utter'. I suspect there are parts of fashionable London where we might still hear it.

It's notable how much of present-day grammatical change is anticipated in the writing of these earlier authors. The case of the progressive form of the verb (p. 167) is an example. While there has been a definite speeding up of the change in the last half-century, the progressive has been slowly and steadily making progress over the past 200 years. The traveller and archaeologist Lady Gertrude Bell writes to her parents from Baghdad in June 1917:

Oh my dearest ones it's so wonderful here – I can't tell you how much I'm loving it.

Note to McDonald's: Lady Bell was there first.

Keyword: hypercorrection

The lesson of the past is that grammatical change never stops and, for the most part, continues without people noticing it. Few – other than linguists – would have been aware of the changes affecting the progressive, for example. Trouble arises only in a prescriptive climate, when a change conflicts with the rules laid down in the grammars. So, for example, there has been a long-standing conflict over the choice of pronouns following forms of the verb *to be*. The eighteenth-century grammars insisted that pronouns should be in their subject form (the nominative case in Latin) not the object form; so it was correct to say *It is I* and *It is he* and incorrect to say *It is me* and *It is him*, notwithstanding the fact that the latter forms have been in use since the sixteenth century. Macbeth calls: 'And damned be him that first cries, "Hold, enough!"' The fact that the grammarians were so exercised by it shows how popular the object usage must have been.

Why do changes take place? There are several factors, such as *analogy*, the process in language which makes a minority form eventually follow the majority form. *Holp* in Shakespeare has today become *helped*, conforming to the rule that past tenses add -*ed*. Similarly, when pronouns follow a verb or a preposition in English, they take the object form (*She saw me, I spoke to her*), so there is pressure on any verb that doesn't do this to conform to the rule.

That should have been the end of the story of the *I*/*me* usage controversy, but the consequences of the prescriptive insistence are still with us. The heightened sensitivity over the issue made people scared to use *me*, in case they would be criticized. They transferred the fear to a long-standing idiom in English, *between you and me* (*and the gatepost*), leading to the form which is so widespread now that it has even prompted a usage book title: *Between You and I: a Little Book of Bad English* (James Cochrane and John Humphrys, 2003). The ongoing nature of the controversy is reflected in a later title: *Between You and Me: Confessions of a Comma Queen* (Mary Norris, 2015).

The phenomenon is technically called *hypercorrection* – the extension of a supposedly correct form to situations where it would not traditionally be used. (Prepositions have taken the object form since Anglo-Saxon times.) There had already been the occasional hint of this happening before the eighteenth century: Shakespeare uses *you and I* twenty times in his plays, nineteen of them in subject position (as in 'you and I must part'). But in *The Merchant of Venice*, Antonio writes to Bassanio: 'all debts are cleared between you and I'. The construction must have had its idiomatic character even then. However, controversy didn't arise until the era of prescriptivism, when commentators began to point out that what the grammarians were saying was different from what most people were doing. Here's Joseph Priestley, in a section on 'Pronouns' at the end of his *Rudiments of English Grammar* (1761), drawing attention to the change that was taking place:

> Contrary, as it evidently is, to the analogy of the language, the nominative case is sometimes found after verbs and prepositions. It has even crept into writing. *The chaplain intreated my comrade and I to dress as well as possible.*

But he is no prescriptivist:

All our grammarians say, that the nominative cases of
pronouns ought to follow the verb substantive as well
as precede it; yet many familiar forms of speech, and the
example of some of our best writers, would lead us to make
a contrary rule; or, at least, would leave us at liberty to
adopt which we liked best.

And he then quotes Addison ('It is not me you are in love
with'), Swift ('It cannot be me'), and others. 'To adopt which
we liked best' – a maxim which went against all that prescriptivism stood for, but which gets a much more sympathetic
reception today, except from the self-appointed grammar
guardians.

These examples illustrate the second reason for the unfin-
ished – unfinishable – state of English grammar: changes in
usage, and changes in attitudes towards usage, require constant monitoring. Who knows which of the three positions
will eventually become the grammatical norm? In a century's
time, will everyone be saying and writing *between you and me*
or *between you and I*, or will a stylistic option have become
established, with the *I* form used in formal communication
and the *me* form in informal? Or will the controversy still
be rumbling on, as it has over the past two centuries? For
linguists, the uncertainty is part of a normal scenario of language change, and a large part of the attraction in studying
the subject.

24

Going transatlantic

We can never be definite about our linguistic future. Language reflects society, and any grammatical futurologist has to be simultaneously a social and political futurologist. No Anglo-Saxons would have been able to predict the changes that altered the character of their language so dramatically. No medieval scholars would have dared suggest that, one day, virtually nobody would know Latin. And today, who could say what character English grammar will have in a thousand years' time?

One trend we can be sure about: languages and dialects will continue to influence each other, as they always have. The mutual influence manifests itself most noticeably in vocabulary, as we can see everywhere in the thousands of loanwords that have entered English over the centuries. But it affects grammar too. Grammar is bigger than any one person's usage, or the usage of any one community. The earliest English manuscripts show many local dialect differences, and as English has spread, so these differences have multiplied. We can see the increase in the way the standard English grammar of the verb *to be* has been complemented by many nonstandard forms. To take just one: the alternative ways of saying *you are*, when addressing a single person. *The Linguistic Atlas of England* shows *ye are* in Northumberland, *thou are* in Lancashire, *thou art* in Derbyshire, *thee art* in Cornwall, *thou is* in Yorkshire, *you be* in Sussex, *you bin* in Shropshire, and *thee bist* in Gloucestershire, along with several other locations. This was published in 1978. Immigrant usage has since increased the variation with such forms as *you is* and omission of the verb (*you beautiful*).

The grammatical variation we hear as we move from place to place in England is also noticeable as we move around the world. In particular, the differences between American and British grammar have long been recognized. There aren't very many points of difference but some can cause occasional problems of comprehension, and even when there is no problem of understanding they can attract a strong reaction, especially in Britain, where there has been a traditional dislike of Americanisms. Henry Alford, author of *The Queen's English* (1860), bemoans 'the process of deterioration which our Queen's English has undergone at the hands of the Americans', and his gloom is echoed by many a modern pundit. But not all features of American grammar have arrived in Britain (or, for that matter, in other varieties of English), as will be evident from the following selection showing the range of grammatical difference. I'll illustrate them according to word class, and in each pairing I'll note the American usage first.

Nouns

Very few differences affect the noun phrase. A tiny group of nouns have different numbers, such as *math – maths, an inning – an innings, accommodations – accommodation*. The definite article varies in *at the university – at university* and *in the hospital – in hospital*. Nouns with a group meaning, such as *government, committee,* and *team* are usually singular in AmE (*The committee has met, Our team has won*), but can also be plural in BrE. When Brits say *The committee has made up its mind,* they're thinking of the committee as a single entity; when they say

The committee have made up their minds, they're thinking of the committee as a collection of individuals.

Verbs

Far more variations affect verbs, but the situation is more complex because the contrasts aren't usually straightforward. For instance, non-Americans notice *dove* for *dived*, and might not realize that Americans also say *dived*. They notice *ate* rhyming with *mate* instead of *met*, forgetting that the pronunciation is also common in some British regional accents. The same point applies to *Our team was beat* [=beaten], also heard regionally outside the USA. And although past-time forms such as *burned, learned,* and *smelled* are usually spelled with *-ed* in AmE, contrasting with *burnt, learnt,* and *smelt* in BrE, the *-ed* forms are found in Britain too. There's a subtle difference of meaning. An event with a long duration is likely to be spelled with *-ed*: *The fire burned for three days.* A sudden event is likely to be spelled with *-t*: *I burnt the toast.*

The American usage that most often confuses British people is *gotten*, because they don't understand the rules governing its use in AmE. It's used only after the auxiliary verb *have*, and it can't be used in the sense of 'possess'. So these sentences are acceptable AmE:

We've gotten off at the wrong stop.
They've gotten into difficulty.

and these aren't:

We gotten very drunk yesterday.
She's gotten red hair.

British youngsters trying to copy American speech often get it wrong. Maybe they should read some Chaucer first, for they would find *gotten* there, following the same rules, as seen in these lines from 'L'amant' in *La Belle Dame Sans Mercie*:

By which love *hath* of enterprise notable
So many hertes *gotten* by conquest.

Several usages, now considered American, were in British English first.

The use of some auxiliary verbs changes too. For BrE *I shan't object*, we find AmE *I won't object*. For BrE *You ought to take more care*, we find AmE *You want to (wanna) take more care*. For BrE *You needn't bother*, we find AmE *You don't need to bother* (also heard in Britain, of course). This use of *do* is typical of many contrasts, one of which has often caused transatlantic confusion. In a somewhat old-fashioned BrE we'll hear sentences like *I haven't an umbrella* and *Has he a car?* These would be highly unlikely in AmE, where we'd find *I don't have an umbrella* and *Does he have a car?* BrE does the same these days, of course, so I don't suppose the old ambiguity would arise any more:

American visitor to British lady: Do you have children?
British lady: Not very often.

BrE also has an informal construction with *got* (*I haven't got an umbrella, Has he got a car?*) which would be unusual in AmE.

Some other points of contrast involving verbs (BrE first):

I've just eaten. – I just ate.
I'd like you to read this. – I'd like for you to read this.
Go and tell the manager. – Go tell the manager.
I suggested they should leave. – I suggested they leave.
How is it that you never asked them? – How come you never asked them?

Many of these contrasts are diminishing, especially among young people in Britain, as a result of increasing exposure to AmE in the media. I hear *How come?* all the time these days.

Adjectives and adverbs

Other word classes also show notable differences, and these are among the ones that most often attract criticism by purists in Britain. Chief among these is the use of adjectives where BrE would use adverbs:

> Drive safe. – Drive safely.
> That's real nice. – That's really nice.
> You did good. – You did well.
> I sure like … – I really like …

Of course, if you're a Briton consciously trying to be a 'cool dude', these are the kind of usages you will adopt. And – though it's much less common – any American wanting to sound British would go in the other direction.

Some AmE usages have now become widespread in BrE. Buddy movies and TV series, such as *Friends*, popularized *you guys* as an informal plural pronoun of address, and I hear it everywhere now. It's a useful way of reducing the potential abruptness of the bare pronoun, and adding rapport. Compare:

> Would you mind if I shut the window?
> Would you guys mind if I shut the window?

Good as an alternative response to *How are you?* is another example.

> How are you? I'm good.
> How are you? I'm well.

The point to appreciate is that these aren't synonymous. *I'm well* refers to my state of physical health. *I'm good* refers to my mental well-being. It's a new semantic contrast, and, judging by the frequency with which we hear it, one that meets a need.

Prepositions

There are several prepositional contrasts, some used in formal writing as well as informal speech:

Let's sit toward the front. – Let's sit towards the front.
I got off of the bus. – I got off the bus.
The tree is in back of the house. – The tree is behind the house.
I have a house on New Street. – I have a house in New Street.
It's a quarter of three. – It's a quarter to three.
It's twenty after three. – It's twenty past three.
He was named for his grandfather. – He was named after his grandfather.
I'm there Monday through Thursday. – I'm there from Monday up to and including Thursday.
Let's meet Tuesday. – Let's meet on Tuesday.
Shop HMV for the best bargains! – Shop at HMV for the best bargains!

Again, the contrasts are not always mutually exclusive. Many Americans say *quarter to three,* for example; and many British now say *Let's meet Tuesday.* Shorter forms have an intrinsic appeal – which is why I think the *through* usage is bound to become universal one day, replacing the wordy *up to and including Thursday* or *up to Thursday inclusive.*

Not a big deal

The differences between American English and other world varieties of English are always the first ones to be cited when talking about international regional differences in grammar, because the global influence of the USA has been so marked during the twentieth century. The antipathy towards uncontrolled Americanisms in Britain is often heard in other English-speaking countries, though adverse reactions tend to diminish over time. Familiarity always eventually breeds linguistic content. Items that were being pilloried as American a century ago are never commented upon today. In the 1860s, people were objecting to *enjoyable, reliable,* and *recuperate*. Here's *Punch* sounding off about *recuperate* in its issue of 9 January 1864:

> How can people who call themselves members of the
> Anglo-Saxon family use such language? As for you who
> owe allegiance to HER MAJESTY, and are in duty bound to
> maintain the purity of the QUEEN's English; consider all
> such English as 'Recuperate' President's English, spurious,
> base, villainous; pray you, avoid it.

Even if the reaction is not one of antipathy, there is nonetheless a proper respect for identity. An American edition of a British book may insist on grammatical changes, and vice versa. We might expect this in non-fiction texts appearing in both British and American editions, but it can happen in fiction publishing too. Put the UK and US editions of the Harry Potter books side by side, and several of the grammatical changes noted in this chapter appear. For example, we see BrE *shan't* changed to *won't, whilst > while, have got > have gotten, next day > the next day, he's got flu > he's got the flu, at weekends > on weekends,* and *September the first > September first*. Even idioms are affected: *was hard-done-by > had it bad*. My favourite example is in Chapter 3 of *The Chamber of Secrets*: *Bit rich coming from you*, says British Harry to Ron. *You should talk*, says American Harry.

Of all the changes in a series like this, the vast majority affect vocabulary – *sweets* becoming *candy*, that sort of thing. The grammatical changes are relatively few. And indeed, when we calculate all the points of grammatical difference between AmE and BrE, in all sources, we don't get a very large total. Of the 3,500 or so index entries in *A Comprehensive Grammar of the English Language* (p. 118), only a few dozen are flagged up as showing a difference between AmE and BrE – that's just one or two per cent. So it's definitely not the case, as far as grammar is concerned, that the two nations are 'divided by a common language' (as Oscar Wilde, George Bernard Shaw, and Winston Churchill are all supposed to have said).

Interlude: Another pretty little Americanism

ANOTHER PRETTY LITTLE AMERICANISM.

Englishman (to Fair New-Yorker). "MAY I HAVE THE PLEASURE OF DANCING WITH YOU!"
Darling. "I GUESS YOU MAY—FOR I CALC'LATE THAT IF I SIT MUCH LONGER HERE, *I SHALL BE TAKING ROOT!*"

Punch, *31 May 1864, p. 210*

25
Going global

Why are there grammatical differences at all? It is all to do
with the way language communities evolve. People speak like
each other in a community for the obvious reason that they
want to understand each other, but also for the less obvious
reason that they want to bond with each other, and to achieve
an identity that distinguishes them from other communities.
And when they move away from that community, and join –
or, in the case of America, begin – another one, it doesn't take
long before they start to speak differently, both in pronunciation (accent) and in grammar and vocabulary (dialect).

Within a few decades of the settlers from England arriving
in North America, in the seventeenth century, visitors were
commenting on a distinctive American voice – the result of
a melting pot of the different accents and dialects spoken
by the new arrivals, who came from many different parts of
Britain. The same thing happened some time later in Australia, New Zealand, Canada, and the Caribbean, as new cultural
identities developed. And when in the twentieth century
independence was achieved in former British colonies, such
as India, Nigeria, and Singapore, a new wave of local Englishes arose, as the communities, anxious to develop a fresh
identity for their new-found independence, made local adap-
tations to the English that had been part of their lives for so
long. The expression 'New Englishes' reflects the prolifer-
ation of these modern varieties. They are chiefly identified, as

with American and British English, through their distinctive accent and vocabulary, but grammar plays a part too.

The kinds of grammatical change that have taken place are very similar to those already seen between British and American English, but it isn't usually so easy to identify where a usage comes from. Try these five examples, all taken from recent issues of the journal *English Today*.

If you saw a sign in a metro station saying 'Mind the gaps'?

You could be in Shenzhen in southern China, just over the border from Hong Kong, in the Beijing subway, or in a few other Chinese cities, where this English expression glosses a notice in Chinese. Londoner underground-travellers are, of course, familiar with the sound of 'Mind the gap', as they enter or leave a train. Why the change? Chinese doesn't make a distinction between singular and plural noun forms, and as there are many gaps on the platforms, they see nothing wrong with using the plural here. It sounds odd to Londoners' ears, of course, because they're used to the singular form. Anyone visiting China who might think of it as an error is missing the point: the usage is well established as part of a local standard now, just as *accommodations* is in American English.

If you heard someone say 'Where you going, la?'

You could be in Singapore, Malaysia, or various other parts of South East Asia. The use of the particle *la* at the end of a sentence is widespread, along with other particles such as *lo* and *ma*. *La* acts as a bonding feature between the speakers. It shows they are in rapport, speaking informally, being amicable. *OK* as a response could sound a bit abrupt. *OK, la* adds a warmer tone. The closest we get to this in British or North American English is when speakers add a friendly *eh* at the end of a sentence – something that is very common in Canada.

If you read in an examination paper 'A school-boy was knocked down by a speeding car. My father picked him. He rushed him to hospital.'

You could be in Uganda. The example was indeed part of an English-language paper set by the Ugandan Examinations Board a few years ago, and the exercise the students had to perform was to use connectives to make a single complex sentence. In traditional standard English we would have to say *My father picked him up*; but the omission, addition, or substitution of a different particle is common in Ugandan English. We also find *to fill the forms* (instead of *fill in* or *fill out*), *to air out one's views* (instead of *to air one's views*), and *to break off for holidays* (instead of *break up*).

If you heard someone say 'I'm after giving him a lift'

You would be in Ireland, where the presence of a construction in Irish Gaelic grammar has influenced Irish speakers of English since at least the seventeenth century. It's been described as the 'hot news' use of a verb, as it reports an action that has been completed very near to the moment of speaking. In the example, the lift has just taken place. The usage isn't heard with equal frequency everywhere: it's much more common in the Republic of Ireland than in Northern Ireland, for example. There are also instances of it being used to refer to events that haven't yet been completed, such as *Where's Mike? He's after going to Dublin* – where Mike has begun his journey and is still travelling.

If you heard someone say 'She's been admitted in a hospital'

You could be in Cameroon, where movement to an enclosed place is usually expressed by *in*, rather than the *into* or *to* heard in traditional standard English. Similarly, people *go in a house* or *send an announcement in a radio station*. The usage is logical enough: the place being entered is enclosed, so that literally we are 'in' it. In fact, such a usage is often found in earlier English – the *OED* has examples from as early as 1300 ('In a castel he entred thare') – and several other countries display the same use of this preposition. I recall being greeted with 'Welcome in Egypt' by the director of the British Council there.

As few descriptive studies have been made, it's always possible that any of the above usages could be encountered in other parts of the English-speaking world. Indeed, some grammatical features, which would definitely be nonstandard in traditional standard English, have taken place in so many territories where English is routinely used that it's no longer possible to identify them with particular countries, such as Cameroon or Malaysia, or even with a particular region or continent. Rather, they are features of an emerging generalized 'English as a lingua franca', used as a foreign language by educated people in all sorts of settings, including academic conferences, business meetings, and radio or television broadcasts.

Take, for example, the difference between countable and uncountable nouns. Countable nouns like *book, table,* and *egg* can be used as singulars and plurals, and with the indefinite article (and numerals, of course): *the books, a book, three books*. Uncountable nouns, such as *advice, research*, and *music*, don't vary in this way: we don't say *the advices, an advice, three advices*. But this is precisely what we do find when we listen to the way English is spoken as a foreign language, all over the world. The speakers will have been taught the traditional rule about the way uncountable nouns work, but they seem instinctively drawn to making these nouns countable, for they talk about *advices, furnitures, homeworks, underwears, researches, informations, musics*, and so on, and say such things as *What a bad luck*.

Prescriptively minded people worry about this, saying that changes of this kind are altering the grammatical character of the language. Yes they are, but the historical evidence tells us that this is nothing new. We see Chaucer talking about *wise informations and teachings*. Coverdale's Bible has *informations and documents of wisdom*. In the eighteenth century, we find Lord Chesterfield writing a letter saying *The informations I have received*. Rather than *informations* being a novelty, it seems that it has always been there, awaiting rediscovery. English is more tolerant of variations between countable and uncountable nouns than prescriptive grammarians think.

The *OED* is the place to go to find examples of uncountable nouns being used in a countable way. It shows philosopher David Hume in 1752 observing that 'these researches may appear painful and fatiguing'. Essayist Richard Steele in 1709 wrote that he would publish 'such my Advices and Reflections'. Edmund Spenser in 1590 wrote about someone going to prepare 'his furnitures'. And Cloten (in Shakespeare's *Cymbeline*, 2.3.38) complained about how he had assailed Innogen 'with musics'. Clearly, the usage of nouns as countable or uncountable has been vacillating for a very long time, so it's hardly surprising to find ongoing change in the new varieties of English emerging around the world.

The two billion people who speak English these days live mainly in countries where they've learned English as a foreign language. There are only around 400 million mother-tongue speakers – chiefly living in the UK, Ireland, USA, Canada, Australia, New Zealand, South Africa, and the countries of the Caribbean. This means that for every one native speaker of English there are now five non-native speakers. The centre of gravity in the use of English has shifted, therefore. Once upon a time, it would have been possible to say, in terms of number of speakers, that the British 'owned' English. Then it was the turn of the Americans. Today, it's the turn of those who have learned English as a foreign language, who form the vast majority of users. Everyone who has taken the trouble to learn English can be said to 'own' it now, and they all have a say in its future. So, if most of them say such things as *informations* and *advices*, it seems inevitable that one day some of these usages will become part of international standard English, and influence the way people speak in the 'home' countries.

Those with a nostalgia for linguistic days of old may not like it, but it will not be possible to stop such international trends. Even countries that have established academies to 'protect' their languages have been unable to stop language change. Dr Johnson's comment about trying to 'lash the wind' comes to mind (p. 166). And these days, the pace of change has increased because of the close linguistic encounters that have been enabled through the Internet.

Interlude: A good good example

One of the most fascinating grammatical features in many languages is the way a word is repeated to intensify the meaning. The phenomenon is called *reduplication*.

This happens quite a lot in standard English. We say that something is *very very nice* or that it is a *no-no*. Sometimes the repetition acts as a kind of exaggeration, as when we describe a costume as *pretty-pretty* – meaning 'excessively pretty'. Sometimes it softens the force, as with *bye-bye* and *night-night*, which are more intimate and informal than the simple *goodbye* and *goodnight*. We would say *Goodnight, ma'am*, when addressing the Queen, but not (usually) *Night-night, ma'am*.

One of the most noticeable features of world Englishes is their use of reduplication in ways that go well beyond what we encounter in standard English. In Singapore, you'll hear people saying that things are *small small*, meaning 'very small'. In Nigeria, if you are *well well*, you are 'very well'. If you *look look* at someone, you are staring ('looking a lot').

Indian Pidgin English is an example of a variety that uses reduplication in a remarkable number of ways. The emphatic function is there in *They give money very very*, which means 'a lot of money'. But when we hear *This book is fifty fifty year old* the repetition conveys a sense of wonder. Someone who greets you with *Good good morning* is adding a note of intimacy. And if you hear *This house has small small room* the meaning is not 'a very small room' but 'several small rooms'. The reduplication expresses plurality. There's no *-s* ending because speakers feel that the reduplication already conveys the idea of 'more than one'. And if there were a very large number of small rooms, the reduplication could continue: *This house has small small small room*. It may sound a primitive way of talking, but actually it's not so different from standard English – something I find very very very interesting.

26

Grammar online

Before the Internet arrived, it was difficult to see how a local English grammatical usage in, say, Singapore, could ever have made an impression on the world English stage. How would it ever have been noticed, outside of that country? Relatively few people would have had the opportunity to visit Singapore, and relatively few Singaporeans would have taken up residence in an English-speaking country, so exposure to any distinctive local usage would have been sporadic and inconsequential. Radio and television were the first media to give some of the new Englishes an international presence, through occasional films, documentaries, and comedy series – I'm thinking of series such as the BBC's *The Kumars at No. 42*, which twice won an International Emmy (2002 and 2003) and a Peabody Award (2004). But nothing matches the global reach of the Internet.

Thanks to electronic communication, all major global varieties of English are now routinely accessible. We no longer have to visit a country to read its English newspapers or listen to its English radio broadcasts; and in the forums that drive social media we can meet people from any country, and be exposed to their geographical identity through their use of local English vocabulary, spelling, pronunciation – and grammar. Often there's a problem in working out where they're from, because so many of the participants are anonymous or linguistic cross-dressers; and in a setting such as a Wikipedia entry, with its mixed and multiple authorship, it's never possible to be sure about the origins of grammatical idiosyncrasies. But most websites and blogs do display their provenance, and with an enterprise as large as the Web, there's more than enough data from individual English-speaking countries to glut any grammarian's appetite.

So, if I want to find out at first hand what is happening to grammatical usage in India, for example, and whether written English there is being affected, all I have to do is call up a copy of a local newspaper and read a selection of articles. The language will be formal, and largely reflect standard British usage, of course, but every now and again it will be possible to spot a grammatical difference that suggests what is happening in Indian English as a whole. While writing this paragraph I looked up *The Times of India* and read the main political article of the day, in which I found 'public facilities like education and health are in a disarray' (rather than 'in disarray') and, a few lines later, that a former prime minister had 'lost deposit' (rather than 'lost his deposit'). The previous two chapters have shown that such variations in noun phrases are among the expected areas of dialect difference. Before the advent of the Internet, it would have been difficult to find examples like these so easily.

Grammatical change online?

But what is happening in the traditional heartlands of English? Is the Internet influencing the grammar of the standard language in Britain, the USA, Australia, and other first-language territories? There's a pervasive myth that electronic communication is having a harmful influence on languages, but when we look closely at the structure of the sentences we read (or hear) online, we find no such thing. In fact, we see hardly any difference at all.

The English syntax and morphology that we see in websites, emails, blogs, social media, and other Internet outputs is not noticeably different from what we saw in pre-Internet days. No new word orders have entered the language as a result of the Internet, and word-endings have remained the same, despite some early experiments. I recall the jocular extension of the *-en* plural in *oxen* to other words ending in *-x* (as in *boxen* and *matrixen*). And there was the use of a new *-z* plural to suggest illegal downloads (as in *tunez* and *filmz*) in the early days when people failed to appreciate the seriousness of online piracy. Neither have much Internet presence now.

The most obvious novelties relate to the use of punctuation to mark constructions, where many of the traditional rules have been adapted as users explore the graphic opportunities offered by the new medium. We see a new minimalism, with marks such as commas and full stops omitted; and a new maximalism, with repeated use of marks as emotional signals (*fantastic!!!!!!*). We see some marks taking on different semantic values, as when a full stop adds a note of abruptness or confrontation in a previously unpunctuated chat exchange. And we see symbols such as emoticons and emojis replacing whole sentences, or acting as a commentary on sentences. The topic deserves a chapter to itself – but that would be to repeat what I have written in my book *Making a Point*.

Although the formal character of grammar has been (so far) unaffected by the arrival of the Internet, there have been important stylistic developments. Short-messaging services, such as text messaging and Twitter, have motivated a style in which short and elliptical sentences predominate, especially in advertisements and announcements:

Talk by @davcr Wednesday 8 pm Holyhead litfest.
Grammar matters – dont miss.

The combination of shortening techniques plus the use
of nonstandard punctuation makes it difficult at times to
assign a definite syntactic analysis to the utterance. We often
encounter a series of sentential fragments:

get a job? no chance still gotta try – prob same old same
old for me its a big issue or maybe Big Issue lol

We get the gist, but only the tweeter would be able to tell us
whether, for example, the phrase *for me* goes with the preceding construction or the following one. On the other hand, the
140 characters of Twitter are sufficient to allow sentences of
25 or 30 words, so we also find messages that are grammatically regular and complex, with standard punctuation:

I'll see you after the movie, if it doesn't finish too late.
Will you wait for me at the hotel entrance where we met
last time?

Long-messaging services, such as blogging, where there is no
limitation on the number of characters, have allowed a style
of discourse characterized by loosely constructed sentences
that reflect conversational norms. Nonstandard grammatical choices now appear in formal written settings (print on
screen) that would never have been permitted in traditional
written texts, where editors, copy-editors, and proofreaders
would have taken pains to eliminate them. When writing a
blog, or sending a tweet, there is no copy-editor looking over
your shoulder to correct your grammar. Here's an example of
the kind of thing that happens.

Blends

Blogs display lots of syntactic blends – the conflation of two types of sentence construction. Here are some simple blends I've seen online:

> For which party will you be voting for in the March 9 election?
> From which country does a Lexus come from?

In each case, we have a blend of a formal sentence, where the preposition goes in the middle, and an informal one, where it goes at the end:

> For which party will you be voting? / Which party will you be voting for?
> From which country does a Lexus come? / Which country does a Lexus come from?

Syntactic blends arise when people are uncertain about which construction to use – so they use them both. They are very common in speech. It's an unconscious process, which operates at the speed of thought. We rarely see them in writing because copy-editors have got rid of them, but they surface quite often online, where such controls are absent. The uncertainty in the above cases has probably arisen because the writers have been confused in the past by the usage controversy over end-placed prepositions (p. 95).

In this next example, the blend is more difficult to spot, unless you try reading it aloud:

> Although MajesticSEO have already entered into the browser extension market with their release of their Google Chrome extension, the news that their release on Monday will open up their services to Mozilla Firefox

browser users, giving them even quicker access to the information that they receive while using the tool.

Something goes horribly wrong when we reach *users*. We need a finite verb to make this sentence grammatical. It has to be *gives them* or *is giving them* or *will give them*, or the like. The problem here is that the writer has used a very long subject (*the news ... users*, seventeen words), so by the time he gets to the verb he's forgotten how the sentence is going. He evidently thinks that the sentence began at *their release on Monday*, where a non-finite *giving* would be acceptable.

the release ... gives them even quicker access ...
their release on Monday will open up their services to Mozilla Firefox browser users, giving them even quicker access ...

What is semantically most important in the writer's mind (the news of the release) has taken priority over the grammatical construction.

It's the length of constructions that gets in the way, in cases like this. Once a construction goes beyond the easy limits of working memory capacity, problems arise. If we ignore the grammatical words and focus on only the items with lexical content, we see the writer is trying to deal with nine chunks of meaning:

the news – their release – on Monday – will open up
– their services – to Mozilla Firefox – browser – users
[giving them even quicker access]

This is an awful lot to remember. No wonder the writer loses his way. He can't recall where he's been, and he's anxious to push on to his main point, which is 'quicker access'. So in his mind he starts the sentence all over again. If he'd read it through after writing it, or said it aloud (always a useful strategy), he might have spotted it. Even better, he might have rewritten the whole thing to make two shorter sentences. As it stands, it's a 50-word monster.

Internet grammar in unconstrained settings such as blogs displays many features like blends that would pass unnoticed in everyday conversation, but which would attract criticism if they appeared in formal writing. Because most blogs are personal and informal, we pay little attention to them, as long as the writers get their meaning across. Just occasionally a blend achieves celebrity status, and probably never more so than in the title track for the James Bond movie *Live and Let Die*, performed by Paul McCartney's group Wings:

> When you were young and your heart was an open book
> You used to say live and let live
> (You know you did, you know you did, you know you did)
> But if this ever changing world in which we live in
> Makes you give in and cry
> Say live and let die.

The Internet is the world in which we live in now; but for grammarians it's not only one that presents them with evolving styles and controversial usages. A major impact of the Internet is educational – the way it offers fresh opportunities and methods for the teaching and learning of grammar. Already, many grammar courses exist, aimed at both first-language and foreign-language audiences, of all ages, and the availability of multi-media allows access to all spoken and written varieties of the language. If someone wants a complete online course on English grammar, there is now *The Internet Grammar of English* http://www.ucl.ac.uk/internet-grammar, available online or as an app for Android and

Apple mobile phones. There's also *Englicious* for schools www.englicious.org. It seems we're entering an era of hand-held grammar.

27

Back from the grave

English grammar on the job. English grammar around the world. English grammar on the Internet. The themes and examples of the last eight chapters I hope have shown the relevance of grammar in everyday life, and how discovering more about it can be illuminating, involving, and entertaining. What a contrast with a century ago! The intellectual climate then was so antagonistic to the subject that schools and governments all over the world decided there was no point in teaching it. Schoolteachers soldiered on for a few decades, recycling old textbook material, parsing sentences as a mechanical exercise, teaching a few prescriptive rules that could easily be grasped, and making sure their students could answer the questions about grammar that were still being asked in the main examinations, such as 'underline all the passive verbs in this passage' or 'turn these adjectives into adverbs'. But in the end they gave up. By the mid-twentieth century it had virtually disappeared from classrooms and examinations – and the result was the situation typified by the student's tale I recounted in the introduction to this book.

Why did it lose favour? I gave the answer in Chapter 12: people had become totally fed up with the prescriptive approach to grammar that had dominated nineteenth-century schools. The signs had appeared early on, when the magazine satirists (such as *Punch*) and the literati (such as Dickens and

Hazlitt) began to inveigh against it; and it was not long before the academics weighed in too. In 1868, John Wesley Hales, professor of English literature at King's College London, wrote a savage account of 'the vulgar grammar-maker' who, 'dazzled by the glory of the ruling language, knew no better than to transfer to English the schemes which belonged to Latin'. Two of his paragraphs are worth quoting at length, as they show the strength of feeling that was around at the time:

> He never dreamt that the language for which he was practising his rude grammatical midwifery might have a character of its own, might require a scheme of its own. He knew, or he thought he knew, what the grammar of any language ought to be, and he went about his work accordingly.

> What chance had our poor mother-tongue in the clutch of this Procrustes? The Theseus of linguistic science, the deliverer, was not yet born. So the poor language got miserably tortured, and dislocated, and mangled. Who could wonder if it failed to thrive under such treatment? if it grew haggard and deformed? All the passers-by were on the side of Procrustes; and, when the victim shrieked at some particularly cruel stretch of its limbs, they called it disorderly, reprobate, vicious.

Writers like Hales gradually formed a new climate. The schoolteachers, who were the main means of keeping prescriptivism alive, found themselves increasingly uncomfortable with the Latinate approach, and the government of the day responded to the groundswell of opinion. In 1890, grammar was dropped from the elementary school curriculum in Britain. And in 1910, a Board of Education circular on *The Teaching of English in Secondary Schools* pulled no punches:

In the past the formal teaching of English Grammar was
based on Latin Grammar. It is now recognised that this was
a mistake founded on a whole set of misconceptions.

And it stressed that English 'is a living organism in process
of constant change'.

The view was taken up and expanded in the most influential government report of the period: *The Teaching of English
in England,* chaired by Sir Henry Newbolt, and published in
1921. In its Chapter 9, in a section called 'The problem of
Grammar', we see the nails steadily banged into the grammatical coffin.

Not only do the aims of grammar teaching need restating,
but its methods need radical reform. Nearly all text-books
on grammar are written as if English were a dead language.

Similar things were being said in the USA, Canada, Australia, New Zealand, and other mother-tongue English-speaking
countries. Boards of Education watched each other closely,
and the decisions in one country were soon being copied in
another.

The problem, of course, was what to put in its place. The
Newbolt report asked:

Is it then impossible at the present juncture to teach
English grammar in the schools for the simple reason that
no one knows exactly what it is?

And it answered its own question with a reluctant 'yes':

If by 'English Grammar' be meant a *complete* description of
the structure of the language with special attention to its
differences from other languages, it is certainly far too early
to attempt to teach it.

The reason, it went on, is that 'the linguists [have not yet] finished their work and formulated for us all the rules of modern English speech'. And the report makes a prescient observation:

> What this structure is we are only now beginning to find out. It is possible that future text-books on English grammar will wear an air very strange to those brought up on 'cases', 'declensions', 'conjugations', &c., that we shall hear of new parts of speech and much of 'word-order', 'token words' and the like. But a great deal still remains to be done first.

Indeed. And in the absence of this work, they conclude that English grammar, 'is, when entered upon in the classroom, a territory full of pitfalls'.

Grammar returns – almost

'No one knows exactly what it is'? The irony was that, even in the 1920s, there were some who *did* know what grammar was. The double irony was that most of them were not native English speakers, but scholars in mainland Europe who had taken up the study of English grammar as part of a more general interest in the history of languages. Otto Jespersen – the man who queried the value of defining dogs (p. 139) – was already writing a seven-volume *Modern English Grammar*. This is his manifesto, written in 1909. It clearly sets out the alternative to traditional grammar:

> It has been my endeavour in this work to represent English Grammar not as a set of stiff dogmatic precepts, according to which some things are correct and others absolutely wrong, but as something living and developing under continual fluctuations and undulations, something that is

founded on the past and prepares the way for the future, something that is not always consistent or perfect, but progressing and perfectible – in one word, human.

In the introduction to his abridged version in 1933, he introduces the terminological contrast that has conditioned thinking about grammar ever since:

> The chief object in teaching grammar today ... would appear to be to give rules which must be obeyed if one wants to speak and write the language correctly – rules which as often as not seem quite arbitrary. Of greater value, however, than this **prescriptive** grammar is a purely **descriptive** grammar which, instead of serving as a guide to what should be said or written, aims at finding out what is actually said and written by the speakers of the language investigated, and thus may lead to a scientific understanding of the rules followed instinctively by speakers and writers.

Grammar wasn't dead, it seems, but sleeping. It would wake up, but in a new form.

Jespersen's was the first of several descriptive grammars that came to be written during the century, especially after the growth of linguistics as a university discipline. When I was reading English at University College London, in the early 1960s, I had the choice of half a dozen, of varying sizes, written by American and Dutch grammarians. Then, in 1972, a ground-breaking book was published that introduced a new era: *A Grammar of Contemporary English*, by Randolph Quirk and his associates (p. 118). It was ground-breaking because it was the first grammar to include the early findings of the Survey of English Usage, which had begun its work in 1960 – a grammatical description of all the major varieties of spoken and written British English, based on a large collection of real samples of usage. The Survey included audio recordings and written extracts from all kinds of situations, such as advertising, religion, science, law, and broadcasting, as well as literary genres and everyday conversation of varying levels of formality. Grammar suddenly seemed relevant to everyday life, because the examples used in the description reflected it.

Jespersen was undoubtedly the most influential linguist writing on English grammar in the first half of the twentieth century; but he wasn't an applied linguist – by which I mean he didn't provide pedagogical guidelines to bridge the gap between the detailed descriptions he made and the needs of school students. He assumed that, once a scientific description had been carried out, it would obviously be attractive to everyone, and need no further exposition. Other descriptive linguists would make the same assumption: their job was to describe the language, not to teach it.

But English grammar is an enormous subject. How should teachers select which should be introduced first, and which next? And how should the new approach be taught to them? It did indeed come to pass, as Newbolt predicted, that 'we shall hear of new parts of speech and much of word-order'. This book testifies to that. However, if the new approach were not to fall into the same trap as the old, new ways would have to be found to introduce its terminology smoothly and interestingly. Subjects and objects are not as easy to present to suspicious teachers and students as are cats and dogs.

It was half a century before applied linguists found themselves in a position to address this issue, and to provide an approach to grammar that would renew public and student appeal. Why did it take so long? And why, a century after Jespersen's manifesto, is there still so much uncertainty about the nature and value of grammar? Explanations are needed here too.

28

Why the delay?

It wasn't until the 1990s that most people became aware of the existence of descriptive grammar and schools began to take an active interest in it. Why did it take so long? The most important reason, I think, was the antagonism that had built up towards the teaching of English grammar over the first half of the century. People remembered the boredom and pointlessness of their own grammar-learning days, and assumed that all grammar would be like that. The Newbolt Committee reported an inspector of schools reviewing the situation in elementary schools after grammar was no longer made a compulsory subject: it 'has disappeared in all but a few schools, to the joy of children and teachers'. What a telling denunciation: joy! So when news broke in the 1960s that there were new approaches to grammar being developed, the idea was treated with great suspicion. Teachers in particular were reluctant to go down a road that had once proved to be a dead end. They would take a lot of persuading that there were other roads that could provide better outcomes in oracy and literacy.

But there was another reason for the long delay in presenting new approaches to grammar: the linguists weren't ready with their new roads. Very little research into grammar had taken place at university level before the 1950s. Research projects such as the Survey of English Usage were long-term ventures, and the meticulous description of the many genres of English, in a pre-computer era, was enormously time-consuming. I worked on the London Survey for a while, in the 1960s. Examples of usage from samples of speech and writing were marked up on thousands of slips of paper and filed in large cabinets. No office computers then. Everything was done by hand, including the frequency counts. It would take days to transcribe half-an-hour of recorded speech to ensure that it was accurate, and many more days to analyse it in full. Two research assistants (I was one) would listen to a tape recording and check each other's work. No wonder it took the Survey team over a decade before they felt confident enough to summarize their findings in the form of their first grammar, and another decade before they were able to publish a more comprehensive description.

The result was a huge gap – a wilderness period in which no English grammar teaching existed at all. Those who went to school during the 1970s and 1980s probably never had any lessons on English grammar. The old approach had gone, and the new approach wasn't ready to take its place. Students would pick up odd bits of grammatical terminology if they were learning French or German, and quite a lot if they were learning Latin. As a result, some fortunate souls did come to know what prepositions were. But for most, during that period, grammar was something belonging to their parents' generation – or their grandparents'.

The subject couldn't be totally ignored, as a consequence. Those older generations were now in positions of power. They were the managers in businesses, the senior civil servants in government, the head teachers in schools. They were people who had lived through the grammar-teaching days, and although most of what they had learned had long been forgotten, they did remember some of the prescriptive rules that had been beaten into them. Many of the people who wrote to me when I was presenting my Radio 4 series *English Now* back in the 1980s fell into that category. This correspondent was typical:

> The reason why the older generation feel so strongly about English grammar is that we were severely punished if we didn't obey the rules! One split infinitive, one whack; two split infinitives, two whacks; and so on.

That gentleman was now in charge of a company in which written reports and brochures formed a major part of his business. Doubtless not a single split infinitive would be found in his employees!

This has to be put alongside another group of correspondents, younger and more junior, such as this one from a civil servant:

> I was told to stop splitting infinitives when I'd no idea what an infinitive was, or why splitting them was so important. I began to feel really stupid.

And in the 2000s there's another group who feel just as uncomfortable: parents, who have children going through an education system in which grammar has once again begun to play a part (as explained in my Appendix). This comment is typical:

> I never had any English grammar when I was in school, so when my kids ask me questions about it I can't help them.

These groups now have a double burden: inferiority on top of uncertainty. In such a situation, they look elsewhere for help. And for a while they think they've found it, in what I call the neo-prescriptivist revival.

Do as I say

Despite the repeated criticisms of prescriptivism described in Chapter 12, the approach didn't die out. Although not taught in schools, it remained alive through the recommendations of usage guides, such as those written in the UK by Henry Fowler and Ernest Gowers, or in the USA by William Strunk and E. B. White. Since 2000 they have proliferated. Every year or so we find books appearing in which the authors – sometimes well-known personalities in their own country – take it upon themselves to sort out the uncertainties of English grammar once and for all, just as Bishop Lowth and Lindley Murray did. They present a highly personal account, invariably written in an elegant style and informed by a life-time of professional experience in working with language, but fiercely intolerant of those whose usage differs from their own. And they sell well.

I'm thinking of books such as *Eats, Shoots and Leaves* (2003) by journalist Lynne Truss, *Lost for Words* (2004) by broadcaster and journalist John Humphrys, *Gwynne's Grammar* (2012) by businessman N. M. Gwynne (incorporating William Strunk's *Guide to Style*, originally written in 1918), and *Strictly English* (2010) by journalist Simon Heffer. The subtitles indicate their attitude.

> Truss: *The Zero Tolerance Approach to Punctuation.*
> Humphrys: *The Mangling and Manipulating of the English Language.*
> Gwynne: *The Ultimate Introduction to Grammar and the Writing of Good English.*
> Heffer: *The Correct Way to Write, and Why it Matters.*

Each presents the same argument: do as I say, and you'll be fine. This is why they appeal to the uncertain generation: if someone as important as [CHOOSE A NAME] says what is correct, then if you do likewise your grammatical troubles will be over. It sounds like an elegant and simple solution. And it would be, if they all agreed on their recommendations.

Unfortunately, as was the case with the earlier generations of prescriptivists, this never happens. The personal tastes of the writers result in an inevitable variety of opinions. For example, Heffer thinks splitting an infinitive is 'inelegant' and considers it more 'logical' to keep the *to* next to the verb; Humphrys thinks it is 'a fine example of a bogus rule', and dismisses the logic argument out of hand. So if readers take both books seriously, they have no idea what to do.

Nor would they be any clearer if they restricted themselves to one book and tried to follow its injunctions carefully, as they will be confused by the inconsistencies they see. Heffer, for example, begins his section on the passive by stating clearly: 'In good style, writers should avoid the passive wherever possible.' But on the same page we read (I underline the passives):

> The passive voice of a transitive verb <u>is used</u> to create the form ...
> ... they <u>can be used</u> to create distance ...
> If an active sentence <u>must be turned</u> into a passive, only the main verb need change.

He concludes: 'why anyone should want to turn an active into a passive is beyond me' – having just used three. Faced with a 'do as I say, not as I do' situation, readers are still unclear about how they should behave.

These are journalists, not linguists, and the basic law of journalism, according to John Humphrys (in a diary piece for *The Spectator* in 2006), offering a defence of his position on usage, is: 'First simplify, then exaggerate.' It's a view that might work well for some subjects, but never for language, as the devil, in language, always lies in the detail.

The importance of context

Here's an example of how a lack of attention to detail can get you into trouble. When Lynne Truss's book came out, a reviewer in *The New Yorker* had a happy time pointing out errors of punctuation in her writing. He began with the opening page: 'The first punctuation mistake ... appears in the dedication, where a nonrestrictive clause is not preceded by a comma.' This is the offending passage:

> To the memory of the striking Bolshevik
> printers of St Petersburg who, in 1905,
> demanded to be paid the same rate for
> punctuation marks as for letters, and thereby
> directly precipitated the first
> Russian Revolution

The critic is accusing her of missing the distinction between a restrictive (or defining) and a non-restrictive (non-defining) clause. Truss illustrates this (p. 92) with the following pair of sentences:

> The people in the queue who managed to get tickets were
> very satisfied.
> The people in the queue, who managed to get tickets, were
> very satisfied.

In the first sentence, not everyone got tickets; in the second sentence, everyone did. It's an important grammatical distinction in English, heard in speech through the use of a different intonation and rhythm, and in writing by the presence or absence of commas. Another example, to make the point clear:

> My brother who lives in Canada has sent me a birthday card. (I have more than one brother, and the others don't live in Canada.)
> My brother, who lives in Canada, has sent me a birthday card. (I have just one brother, and he lives in Canada.)

So, on this basis, we would expect a comma after *Petersburg*, as she clearly isn't intending the sentence to be restrictive in its meaning. We can see this if we paraphrase the sentence in this way:

> I'm remembering the St Petersburg printers who precipitated the Revolution (there were other St Petersburg printers who didn't).
> I'm remembering the St Petersburg printers, who precipitated the Revolution (they all did).

This was *The New Yorker* reviewer's point: the sentence needs a comma, and there isn't one. Was it a fair criticism?

This is where the notion of *context* becomes relevant. Context here has three applications: it can refer to the other parts of the discourse surrounding the point at issue (the *grammatical context*); it can refer to our knowledge of what this sentence means (the *semantic context*); and it can refer to the situation which has given rise to the sentence in the first place (the *pragmatic context*). It's the grammatical context that we need to consider first.

Note the effect of adding the parenthetical phrase *in 1905*. It is set off by commas. So if another comma were added, to satisfy the grammatical requirement, the sentence would look like this:

> To the memory of the striking Bolshevik
> printers of St Petersburg, who, in 1905, …

Three commas in a row? For many readers (and publishing houses) this offends against legibility and aesthetics. Truss might simply have omitted the commas around *in 1905*; but, having decided to use them there, the question resolves into: is there any ambiguity by omitting the comma before *who*? Truss's defence would be that there isn't: if we think of this sentence semantically, the only likely interpretation is that all the printers were involved. Only a grammatical pedant, she would probably argue, would insist on a comma when the meaning is so transparent.

As I discussed in Chapter 15, grammar without semantics is sterile, so I would support such a defence. But if we accept the importance of the semantic context in one area of usage, we should accept it in others, and this is what pedants never do. John Humphrys is so incensed by the 'wrong' placement of *only* that when his four-year-old, thinking of taking his toy dinosaurs to school, said *I'm going to take only one*, he got a special hug from his dad. Yet there's no possibility at all that *I'm only going to take one* could be misconstrued, as the spoken stress on the two words (*only* and *one*) links their meanings together, and the meaning is totally clear from the context. The early prescriptive grammarians never noticed the important role that intonation and context plays in making grammar unambiguous, so it's hardly surprising that the point isn't noticed by modern pedants either. And one day, the young Humphrys will pass this rule on to *his* children – unless he has the good fortune to receive some grammar teaching in school from a teacher aware of the inadequacies in the old rule.

Context is critical. To return to Lynne Truss's dedication:

other reviewers might have focused on different punctu-
ational inconsistencies in it. Some would dispute the need
for a comma before *and* – a complicated issue that takes up
a whole chapter in my *Making a Point,* and involves a consid-
eration of such matters as the length of the preceding clause
(that prompts a pause, and thus a comma). Simplifying and
exaggerating won't explain what's going on here. Nor will
it explain the most noticeable punctuation 'error' in the
dedication.

Every time a sentence ends, she says (p. 24), 'there is a
full stop'. It's 'as easy as that'. But there is no full stop at
the end of the dedication sentence, so the matter can't be as
easy as that. Here, her defence would rely on semantic and
pragmatic arguments. Semantic: a dedication is graphically
isolated and doesn't need a mark of sentence ending, as there
is no following sentence with which it might be confused.
Pragmatic: a dedication looks nicer, less cluttered, without
a full stop at the end. Some publishers would give her no
choice in the matter, as it is not part of their house style to
end-point highlighted text. Either way we have an exception
to the rule – and quite a commonly occurring one, as there
are dozens of examples throughout the book.

Context has to be interpreted historically too. The big
fallacy is to interpret the past as if it were the present (what's
been called *presentism*), and to criticize earlier writers for not
taking modern values into account. This kind of linguistic
anachronism is surprisingly frequent. John Humphrys goes
so far as to call the Shakespearean use of *between you and I*
(p. 192) 'the howler to end all howlers!' Poor Shakespeare,
blamed for not anticipating a prescriptive rule that wouldn't
surface until centuries after his death.

The neo-prescriptive movement doesn't solve the problems of grammatical uncertainty. Only an approach which

provides explanations grounded in linguistic realities can do that. But those who present an alternative approach have to live up to the literary standards of the neo-prescriptive writers which, given their professional backgrounds, are very high indeed. Many people buy the above books, not because they are particularly sympathetic to the prescriptive approach or even expecting to be persuaded by it, but simply because they are 'a good read'. And indeed, some of the anecdotes and illustrations of usage, coming from the worlds of broadcasting and journalism, are fascinating, and the commentary often (as with Murray and Lowth, p. 109) illuminating. I, like many others, have enjoyed John Humphrys' affable, lively tone and Lynne Truss's sense of humour, even though the former has called me 'the *capo di tutti capi* ['boss of all bosses'] of the linguistic Cosa Nostra'. He also once called me a 'national treasure', which I thought was very nice, until I reflected: what does one do with national treasures? One locks them up in the Tower of London.

Interlude: Do as I say – government level

We are living at the end of a transitional time. It took the prescriptive approach the best part of half a century to become firmly established in schools. It took a similar period for it to be disestablished, but the memories linger on. The ripples from 250 years of prescriptivism will take a long time to disappear, and the impact of strong personalities can in the meantime turn these ripples into waves. And strong political policies. The way the situation has evolved since the turn of the century illustrates the persistent nature of old-style approaches to grammar, especially when a prescriptive temperament is given political power. This example is from Britain, but parallel cases in other English-speaking countries are not hard to find.

Michael Gove is instructing his civil servants on grammar

This was the headline in the *Independent on Sunday* (21 June 2015). Journalist Mark Leftly went on to describe how instructions posted on the Ministry of Justice intranet, after Mr Gove was appointed Lord Chancellor in May, warned officials about the kind of English they shouldn't be using. Nicholas Lezard in the *Guardian* made a similar point. His headline read: 'Has Michael Gove dreamed up these grammar rules just for our entertainment?' Here are two of the recommendations that were being reported.

1. 'Read the great writers to improve your own prose
   – George Orwell and Evelyn Waugh, Jane Austen
   and George Eliot, Matthew Parris and Christopher
   Hitchens.'
2. The Lord Chancellor has told officials that they must
   not start a sentence with 'however'.

It takes only a few moments searching to find examples of the use of introductory *'However'* in all of these authors, and, of course, in many others too.

> It is her nature to give people the benefit of the doubt. However, Mr. Wickham's account seems to leave no doubt that Mr. Darcy is intentionally unkind. (Austen, *Pride and Prejudice*)

> Celia, now, plays very prettily, and is always ready to play. However, since Casaubon does not like it, you are all right. (Eliot, *Middlemarch*)

The clever journalists, of course, tracked down examples like this one:

> However, I was nudged out of my reverie by the reminder that it was indeed possible to send something through the post on Tuesday and be sure it arrived on Wednesday. (Gove, 2008)

I worry about the time and money spent trying to implement such unreal and self-contradictory prescriptions. But I worry more about the children, who – influenced by the style of their favourite authors – will one day start a sentence with *However* and find themselves at the mercy of a cadre of examiners who would automatically mark it wrong in a national test.

29

A top ten for the future

Looking back over the exploration of grammar in this book, I extract ten basic principles that inform my view of the subject and give it the appeal that motivated my subtitle. I see them as a kind of manifesto for the linguistic approach to grammar.

1. Grammatical change is normal and unstoppable, reflecting the normal and unstoppable processes of social change.
2. Grammatical variation is normal and universal, reflecting the normal and universal diversity of cultural and social groups.
3. A highly diversified society needs a standard grammar to facilitate intelligible supra-regional communication, nationally and internationally. This needs to be respected and studied, and the points of contrast with nonstandard grammar appreciated.
4. A highly diversified society needs nonstandard grammar to enable groups of people to express their regional or cultural identity, nationally and internationally. These features need to be respected and studied, and the points of contrast with the standard grammar appreciated.
5. Neither standard nor nonstandard grammar is homogeneous. Grammatical features are continually subject to the processes of language change, and they display variation arising from the different mediums they

exploit (speech, writing, electronic), the different ranges of formality they employ (informal to formal), and the different occupational domains in which they are used (law, technology, religion, literature, etc.).

6. There is an intimate relationship between standard and nonstandard grammar. Standard grammar users can make use of nonstandard forms, as occasion requires, and nonstandard grammar users can be influenced by the standard in varying degrees. Over time, nonstandard forms frequently influence the way the standard grammar develops and vice versa.

7. Everyone who receives a school education needs to learn to read and write standard English grammar, and to understand its spoken use, because this is the form that carries most prestige in English-speaking national and international society and that gives greatest access to high-status positions at these levels. Some children additionally learn to use standard grammar as a spoken dialect in addition to their mother-dialect; and a small minority, from higher-class backgrounds, use it as a mother-dialect at home. A spoken standard English grammar is the traditional expectation of use in certain careers, such as the civil service, teaching, and national broadcasting.

8. Everyone who receives a school education needs to learn about varieties of nonstandard grammar, because these are the forms that express a person's identity as part of a national or international community and that give greatest insight into community values and attitudes. The first dialect learned by most English-speaking children contains nonstandard grammar, and the importance of this should be recognized when the children arrive in school, respect for it being reinforced

through opportunities to use their home grammar in writing as well as in speech.

9. As English becomes an increasingly global language, we need to reappraise the concept of a single standard English grammar, giving due recognition to the emergence of 'regional standards'. British and American English – the first to emerge at an international level and the source of all other global English varieties – are already well established; and others will follow as the 'New Englishes' of the world acquire local prestige.

10. Grammar is a system of systems, within which we make choices that convey meanings and effects. It should never be studied in isolation from the other properties of language that contribute to meaningful and effective communication – in particular, the perspectives provided by semantics and pragmatics. It is these that show us how to relate structures and uses, take grammar beyond the basic level of 'naming of parts' and mechanical parsing, and point us in the direction of explanations for our grammatical behaviour that are intellectually stimulating and emotionally appealing. In a word, they give grammar its glamour.

Epilogue

They say the penalty of success is when your name is stolen by others for their own purposes. *Hoover* became a generic noun, as did *Sellotape*, *Aspirin*, and *Escalator*. *Google* became an everyday verb. If that is so, then *grammar* has become the most successful word in language study, for virtually every subject has stolen it as a succinct way of describing its fundamental principles and operational structure.

It has been especially popular in book titles. The trend began in the seventeenth century with 'the grammar of military performance' and soon after that 'the grammar of geography'. In the nineteenth century the titles proliferated, with such widely read books as Owen Jones and Francis Bedford's *The Grammar of Ornament* (1856), Charles Blanc's *The Grammar of Painting and Engraving* (1889), and Karl Pearson's *The Grammar of Science* (1892). Since then there have been 'grammars' of poetry, mathematics, society, sabotage, dreams, happiness, trademarks, design, knowledge, identity, computing, and much more. Nor does there seem to be any decrease in its popularity. While I was writing this book (2015) there appeared *The Grammar of Politics and Performance* and, super-ambitiously, *The Grammar of God* – the latter subtitled with the more down-to-earth *A Journey into the Words and Worlds of the Bible*.

In many cases, the allusion to grammar is indirect and metaphorical; but sometimes there is a conscious attempt to apply the term in its linguistic sense to elucidate another intellectual domain. William Charlton's *Metaphysics and Grammar* (2014) is a case in point. His definition of grammar, 'the rules for the construction of sentences out of words', is very close to the one I used earlier in this book. For Charlton, grammar is a sound basis on which to build a metaphysics: it is 'a bridge that takes us from matter to mind'. He argues that by examining sentence functions (statements, questions, commands, counsels ...) we can better understand the issues addressed by metaphysics, such as truth, existence, goodness, change, time, and causation. Grammar, in his view, provides insight into fundamental philosophical questions, such as the difference between truth and falsity; and his approach thus connects us to the views of Aristotle, Plato, and the Stoics, all of whom played a prominent role in the opening chapters of this book.

The English grammar wheel has turned full circle. I was not expecting to end this book with a brief excursus into the world of metaphysics, but there is something rather satisfying in the thought that those who initiated the study of grammar are still playing a part in its story, which continues to unfold in numerous, unpredictable ways.

I miss the good old days when all we had to worry about was nouns and verbs.

An appendix on teaching and testing

Although grammar is of universal relevance and interest, and can be enjoyed for what it is simply by exploring the way a language works, the fact remains that it is almost always first encountered in school, whether in an English class or in a class devoted to learning another language. For those whose responsibility is to teach English, therefore, some further perspective can be helpful.

The role of language acquisition

There's limited time and opportunity for professional development, so if I had to choose one area that would provide greatest help for teachers faced with the need to teach grammar, I would opt for the perspective provided by applying findings from the field of child language acquisition. The stages through which children pass as they master the grammar of their language are fairly well known, as the story of Suzie illustrated, and a more detailed look at each stage can provide many suggestions about how to select and organize grammatical topics. A timeline emerges for word classes, for example: at the earliest stage there's a clear initial focus on nouns and verbs, then on adjectives, adverbs, and prepositions, then determiners and pronouns, and only much later, conjunctions.

Within any one of these categories, we can see a further

developmental ordering: for example, possessive determiners (*my, your*) appear before the general ones (the articles *the* and *a*). This is a useful teaching hint, as the concrete meaning of personal possession helps children to see what determiners do more easily than if they were presented with the more abstract notions of definite and indefinite article. Also more concrete are the determiners *this* and *that*, which express relative distance: *this book* is nearer to me than *that book*.

These determiners can then be used to help get across the meaning of *noun*. Anyone who relies on the traditional definition ('a noun is the name of a person, place, or thing') immediately gets into trouble when they come across words like *music* or *thought*. Is music a thing? Is thought a thing? But they are nonetheless nouns. It's not easy to get around this by trying to add further notional categories to the definition, as these become vague and never-ending ('a noun is the name of a person, place, thing, idea, belief, opinion ...'). The most succinct way is to show how nouns actually work in sentences, such as by drawing attention to the way a noun can be immediately preceded by a determiner: *my mum, my car, my music, my thoughts* ... (Note that *a* is not a good determiner to use here, for there are nouns that do not easily take it – 'uncountable' nouns such as *music, information*, and *furniture*.)

At all stages, children develop a sense of grammar as a system, in which contrasts of meaning are expressed by sets of mutually defining forms. It is, as some linguists have described it, 'a system of systems'. Singular and plural define each other. Present and past tense define each other. Active and passive define each other. The eight personal pronouns define each other. And they all interact in subtle ways. If I choose *he* in a sentence, my listener/reader knows that I am excluding *I, you, she, it, we, they*, and *one* (as in 'One fell off one's horse'). Developing a good sense of pronoun use requires an awareness of what all the options do. There is a choice to be made. What are the different effects of choosing one of the following in an account of an experiment?

> I poured the mixture into the test tube.
> We poured the mixture ...
> You poured the mixture ...
> One poured the mixture ...

Is this why science tends to avoid pronouns altogether? To avoid the personal and make the language more objective?

> The mixture was poured ...

One system leads to another. Now we are exploring the differences between active and passive sentences (p. 127).

An applied linguistic focus also involves exploring the nature of the interactions between teacher and pupil. In the earliest stage of normal child language acquisition, nouns are much more frequent than verbs. Why is this? Presumably because it's easier to grasp what early nouns are: concrete objects such as *doll*, *mummy*, and *dog*. Actions are less easy to perceive: *go*, *do*, *have*. Even the more perceptible actions aren't as easy to identify as we might think. I can draw *doll* or *dog* easily enough; but it isn't so easy to draw *running* or *eating*.

Imagine a scenario now where a child has learned some nouns but is having difficulty learning verbs. This is actually a very common situation with children who have some sort of language delay or disorder. Four-year-old Michael had a vocabulary of about fifty words and was speaking in one-word sentences – a serious delay. Almost all of his words were nouns, and there were no verbs, so correcting this was an early aim of therapy, as verbs are at the heart of clause structure (p. 60). His speech therapist showed him a picture of a girl eating an apple, and asked him 'What's the girl doing?' He answered 'apple', not the expected 'eating'. Another question related to a picture of a boy kicking a ball: 'What's the boy doing?' He answered 'ball'. What is happening here?

The problem lies in the questions the therapist was using, which assume a verb in the answer. 'What doing?' questions, like 'What's happening?' questions, focus on actions, and need a verb for a correct response. So if you are a child who hasn't learned any verbs yet, these are impossible questions to answer. You'll do the best you can, of course, and hope that a noun like *apple* will satisfy the questioner. But then you find that this reply isn't good enough. 'Yes it's a girl,' said Michael's therapist, 'but what's the girl *doing*? She's – ?' Michael looked at the picture and had another go: 'Chair?' The girl was indeed sitting on a chair.

Clearly, in such a situation, Michael needs grammatical help, and this can take many forms. One strategy is for the therapist to use a 'forced alternative' question to focus him on verbs rather than nouns: 'Is she eating or is she drinking?' This is helpful, as it shows Michael the kind of word that he needs to use, but still gives him a bit of a challenge: he has to choose the right verb. It's a strategy that worked well in his case; after answering several such alternatives correctly, he developed his sense of what a verb was to the extent that he began to handle a 'What doing?' question on its own. Now he could have a go at bigger sentences. He was on the clause-learning road.

Grammar across the language-teaching professions

The example from speech therapy illustrates an important

general point: professionals can learn a great deal from each other. Mother-tongue teachers can learn a great deal from the sequencing of grammatical notions presented in speech therapy courses of treatment, or from any series of books for foreign learners of English – and, of course, vice versa. Speech therapists, for example, often use sets of well-designed cards conveying actions, sequences, time-relations, comparisons, and so on, and these can be adapted for other situations. In mother-tongue classrooms there are often colourful posters illustrating various grammatical points, such as word classes or word order. A great deal of this material is now available online; but there is still a serious shortage of case studies which give examples of best grammatical practice.

Awareness of what has been going on in other school subjects can also be illuminating. I know several teachers who have followed the lead of mathematics, and devised grammar tasks that are real and intriguing. In maths teaching, for example, we regularly see such questions as:

Michael bought 7 packs of 8 chocolate bars. How many chocolate bars did he get?
Michael has saved £1.35 in 5p coins. How many 5p coins does Michael have?
In a school of 120 children, only 1/3 are girls. How many boys are in the school?

These take the children into their own daily world. The abstract notions involved – multiplication, division, subtraction – are made concrete and meaningful. Analogously, real-world grammar-oriented questions can be devised, to focus on particular points, such as:

superlatives [showing a picture of three boys and three shirts of different sizes]: Which shirt will fit the tallest boy?

tense contrast [showing pictures of trees in various states of falling and one lying on the ground]: Which tree has fallen down?

Or a spoken language task focusing on order-of-mention (p. 111):

Give this book to Mary after you've given this pen to John.

Dyslexic children in particular find it difficult to follow instructions that break order-of-mention (Chapter 14).

The English Language Teaching (ELT) profession – those who teach English as a foreign language – offers the most extensive array of tried-and-tested examples of grammar used in real-world situations. During the 1960s and 1970s, these teachers experienced a similar process of change to that which was taking place in mother-tongue classrooms. In the latter, the focus on grammatical forms and patterns was over-taken by the 'language in use' movement (p. 134). In the former, a similarly traditional 'grammar-translation' method came to be subordinated to 'communicative' approaches.

The grammar-translation method was the dominant one in classrooms until well into the twentieth century. It derives from the classical approach to the teaching of Latin and Greek, based on a detailed analysis of the written language, and providing exercises in translation, reading comprehension, and the imitation in written work of classical models. Learning mainly involved the mastery of grammatical rules and long lists of literary vocabulary. There was little attention paid to the activities of listening or speaking. As an intellectual discipline, it had a great appeal; but it did little to meet the practical needs of modern language learners. You would learn that the forms of the verb *go* were *I go, I am going,*

I went, I have gone, and so on, but have no knowledge of the situations where, for example, it would be natural to say *I go* as opposed to *I am going,* or *I went* as opposed to *I have gone.* Faced with a real-life situation, that formal grammatical knowledge could let you down – as I discovered with French *tu* and *vous* (p. 137).

Criticism of the grammar-translation method led to the development of several alternative approaches (such as the 'direct method' and the 'audio-lingual method') in which learners were actively involved in speaking and listening to English in everyday situations. In the 'communicative' approach, you would be placed in a real-life situation (such as travelling) and the conversation would be structured in such a way that you would have to understand and use the various forms of the verb appropriately:

Where are you going? I'm going to Bristol.
How are you going to get there? I'm going by bus.
Have you been there before? I went there last year.

In the classroom, teachers would devise 'situational syllabuses', in which real-life interactions were recreated and various linguistic activities practised, such as enquiring, thanking, requesting, complaining, and instructing. 'Notional syllabuses' would focus on the general grammatical concepts that play a central role in language, such as time, duration, and location. The semantic and pragmatic perspectives discussed in Chapters 15 and 16 played a central role in this approach. And, as with mother-tongue teaching, great attention was paid to the role of active choice on the part of the learner.

The parallels in grammar teaching between first- and foreign-language classrooms are at times very striking. Teaching materials often overlap in content, so that ideas from one domain can be used to stimulate activities in the other. An example is a unit in a series called *Skylarks*, a language development programme aimed at six- to nine-year-olds, written by Jeff Bevington and myself, published by Nelson in 1975. Each sentence is accompanied by an appropriately quirky picture:

> Ducks quack, but they can't sing.
> Fish swim, but they don't read books.
> A grasshopper can jump, but it can't count.
> Squirrels climb trees, but they can't paint.
> Most birds can fly, but not many can speak.
> Frogs croak, but they can't play the flute.
> Monkeys climb, but they don't cook.

The sequence ends with:

> Can you cook? Can you count? Can you read? Can you quack?

Compare this with the first two examples from a unit, also strikingly illustrated, in Michael Swan and Catherine Walter's *Cambridge English Course*, Student Book 1, aimed at beginner adult and young adult learners of English as a foreign language, and published by Cambridge University Press in 1984. The unit is called 'Differences'.

> 1. Which of these things can you do? Which of them can't you do?
> Example: *'I can sing, but I can't draw.'*
>
> play chess   speak German
> type   play the violin   drive
> draw   run a mile   sing   play tennis

2. Can you swim / cook / play the piano / dance / go
without sleep / sleep in the daytime?
Ask two other people, and report their answers to the class.
Make sentences with *but*.
'Can you dance?'   'Yes, I can.'
                                   'No, I can't.'
'Diego can dance, but Alice can't.'
'Diego can dance, but he can't cook.'

It's not difficult to see the way ideas from one approach could
inform the other.

Bridging the gap

All language-teaching professions today accept the principle
that there has to be a bridge between structure and use. But
how is this principle actually implemented in the classroom?
An illustration from one educational project shows how the
gap between theory and practice can be successfully bridged.

In 2013–14, I had the opportunity to collaborate with
a local government initiative, in Buckinghamshire, on a
grammar project for the county's schools. An initial training day, introducing several of the notions described earlier
in this book (in particular, the semantic and pragmatic perspectives, p. 125), led to the participating teachers trying
out individual topics in their schools, and devising classroom activities. The children were from Reception classes to
Year 10, in catchment areas ranging from the affluent to the
highly deprived. Some months later, the teachers returned
for another in-service day where they reported on what they
had done, and shared their experience with a second cadre of
teachers who had not been part of the initial day. More classroom work followed, and was reported on in a further in-
service day. The results were then written up as case studies,

along with video reports of the activities, and several are now available online (see p. 266).

Introducing a class to 'adjectives' provides an example of this approach working in practice. What is the very first step? Before introducing *any* new grammatical notion, it's important to check that the pupils don't already know the term, or know it in some other sense. They may have different associations for a word such as *connect*, for example (or *preposition*, as we saw in my introduction). As we saw earlier (p. 84), grammatical metalanguage isn't usually found in pre-school children's speech; but it's nonetheless essential to check that any words needed for the explanation are known, such as – see below – *word* and *describe*.

Here are some of the things that I've seen teachers do, using adjectives as the teaching target.

What is it and what does it do? Identifying and illustrating

- They introduce the term and a definition at an appropriate comprehension level, such as 'an adjective is a word that tells you what someone or something is like' or 'an adjective is a word that describes someone or something'. The semantic approach avoids old-style terminology, such as 'an adjective *qualifies* a noun'.
- They show adjectival use in different parts of a sentence. Adjectives can be used before nouns (*the red car*) and after verbs (*the car is red*). They avoid bringing these terms into the initial definition unless the children are already confident in their use.
- 'We're going on an adjective hunt ...' They compile an adjective dictionary from the words the children already know, as used in their speech and as experienced in their

reading. This might be quite long – Raban's survey (p. 86) found over 400 – so it takes some time. As well as 'obvious' adjectives to do with colour, size, and shape, their speech will contain many dramatic and emotional words such as *silly, naughty, different, horrible, dangerous, careful, rude, delicious, annoying*. In reading, they look out for stories that rely on adjectives, such as *The Enormous Turnip* or *The True Story of the Three Little Pigs*.

• They are ready for the 'awkward' cases that children will propose – the words that are used like adjectives, coming before the noun, but seem to be different in some way. The chief problems here are the ordinal and cardinal numbers, which don't act like adjectives. In particular, they don't compare: we can say *big, bigger, biggest*, but not *four, fourer, fourest*, or *fourth, fourther, fourthest*. Compound nouns where the first element looks like an adjective are another complication: *ironing board, walking stick, running shoes*. The children need to know why they are different: *the big stick* can change into *the stick is big*, but *the walking stick* can't change into *the stick is walking*. And they need to be clear that words like *walking* and *running*, in these examples, aren't being used as verbs.

Trying it out and practising

This means trying out any new piece of grammatical knowledge in all four modes of communication – listening, speaking, reading, and writing. Here are some examples of classroom activities relating to listening and speaking:

Listening

• Telling a story (or just a sentence) which has adjectives

in it, and then telling the same story without the adjectives so that the children hear the different effect.

- Telling a story with the wrong adjective in it, to see if they notice.
- Showing an object and going through a list of possible adjectives, with the class voting on the best ones (taking a leaf out of online forums: like – dislike).

Speaking

- Describing pictures of objects or people, or things in the class (*tall, pretty, skinny, enormous, fat, red-haired …*). This provides an opportunity to show how adjectives can work in sequences – one of their most important characteristics. (Later, they will learn that there are rules governing the order of some adjectives in a sequence.)
- Giving a list of adjectives, and getting them to choose the best ones to describe something. This can provide an opportunity to show how lists work differently depending on where in the sentence they go (*strong, hairy giant – the giant was strong and hairy*).
- Drawing up their own list: say what giants are like (*strong, big, angry, hairy, muscular …*).
- Comparing and contrasting – comparatives and superlatives are already established in spoken language acquisition by age five (*She's bigger than me, I'm the tallest*).
- Playing adjective tennis: two players; umpire provides a noun; player 1 has to think up an appropriate adjective and 'hit' it across to player 2, who has to think up another appropriate adjective and return it to player 1 – and so on, until one player can't think of a further adjective, or uses an inappropriate one, and loses the point. The umpire decides on appropriateness (that

adjective is 'out'). And the player then accepts the decision. Or not. I have seen McEnroe-like altercations – 'You cannot be serious!' – among seven-year-olds, in which one player furiously defends a usage.

That is what does the educational grammarian's heart good: to see two little ones excitedly debating whether a particular adjective is appropriate or not, and using the term without thinking twice about it. Such children are more than ready to transfer their awareness into their reading – for example, discussing why the adjectives are in a story and what would happen if they were changed, or discussing the way they add precision in non-fiction narratives, such as descriptions in natural history or quantities in mathematics (*large, small, even, odd, least, greatest …*). The final step, introducing a wider range of appropriate adjectives into their writing, needs little prompting.

What can be done with adjectives can be done with any grammatical topic. Spread gently over the years of the curriculum, it is then easy to understand the reaction of one of the children in the Buckinghamshire Grammar Project, who came out of a national grammar test and remarked dismissively to her teacher: 'All we had to do was draw circles around things!' It must be like turning up for a driving test, after all those lessons, and being asked simply: 'Can you tell me which is the accelerator?' 'Correct. You've passed.' The conclusion, as stated on the Buckinghamshire website, is unequivocal:

> When taught in context, focused on 'real' language and closely linked to the children's needs, the teaching of grammar can not only improve the quality of their writing, but also their levels of engagement.

Most teaching ideas in language revolve around the notion of *choice* – the central concept in Chapter 16. The children are being systematically taught to recognize the grammatical *options* that the language makes available to them; and it is this emphasis on choosing options that drives all pedagogical grammar projects. The Buckinghamshire team conclude their page of 'key findings' in this way:

> Above all, remember the Grammar Mantra:
> - What options were available?
> - Why was this one chosen?
> - What impact does it have on the audience?

It is a mantra that should be on the walls of all classrooms – and in the offices of grammar test designers.

Progress in grammar teaching is thus being made, in all the language-teaching professions. Certainly it is not the case, as pedantic popular wisdom claims, that 'children don't get taught grammar any more'. On the contrary: there's more grammar being taught in some schools these days than at any time since the 1960s. But provision is patchy, as it has been left up to individual local governments, schools, English departments, and teachers whether to spend time and money doing it – an especial problem when so many teachers have had no training in the subject. The actual amount of grammar being taught varies enormously, particularly at higher levels.

This is where national tests are valuable: they help to even out the situation, while offering pupils a genuine opportunity to show how their grammatical knowledge enhances their linguistic skills (as long as the tests reflect the way grammar is put to use in the real world). When a country starts to test grammar, it has an immediate side effect: it brings the subject to the attention of the teaching profession, and to parents, in a way that most of them have never experienced before.

Testing

It's very difficult to test grammar well, as many of the questions don't have neat yes/no answers, and those that have a straightforward answer are usually not very informative about a child's grammatical ability. Many old-style tests, and some modern ones, do little more than ask students to identify a grammatical point, without giving them any chance to explain why it is there:

> Circle all the adverbs in the sentence below.
> Circle the preposition in the following sentence.
> Which sentence is the passive form of the sentence above?

There is, of course, nothing intrinsically wrong with the directive 'Circle the X', any more than there is – to revert to my car-driving analogy (p. 253) – with the driving instructor's pointing out the brake or the accelerator. What is wrong is if children do nothing with the knowledge they have acquired. We quickly learn what to do with the brake and the accelerator, as we begin to drive the car. What was unsatisfactory about old-style grammar teaching was that, having been told the linguistic equivalent of a brake (an adjective, a passive), learners were given no guidance about what to do with it. They weren't shown how to drive the language anywhere. Nor were they shown the interesting linguistic places they could drive to. Many modern tests fall into the same trap. They fail to explore a child's awareness of grammar in context – the link between structure and use (Chapter 17). The point was repeatedly emphasized by the school inspectors with whom I worked in the 1990s, for example in relation to passives: don't just circle a passive, but *say why it is there*. What does a passive add to the genre in which it is being used? What would be lost if it were replaced by an active?

Since the 1990s, questions of this kind have begun to be explored in classrooms. Students are taught how to 'drive' passives, or connectives, or adjectives – how to recognize them and evaluate their meaning and effect in listening and reading, and how to use them meaningfully and effectively in speaking and writing. And as with cars, there are five stages through which a learner moves:

> What is it and what does it do?
> Can I see you try it out?
> Can I try it out myself?
> Can I practise until I can do it better?
> Can I take a test to show I've mastered it? Please.

That's the point: you *want* to take the test because it acknowledges your competence and gives you a sense of achievement. And, if you've been properly trained, you know you can pass it. In the same way – nerves aside – a grammar test really ought to be easy, if the training has gone well.

A useful preparatory technique is to explore the different ways in which a grammatical topic might be tested. How, for example, might a child's knowledge of adjectives be tested, in the early stages of teaching grammar? The choices range from a very simple (and thus easily markable) identity task to the more advanced (less easily markable) and increasingly open-ended tasks.

1. Identify the target term:
   Draw a circle around the adjectives in the following sentence:
   My thirsty dog drank all the cold water in her red bowl.

2. Make a choice from a set of adjectives, with the child
   shown where they should go:
   Fill each blank with an adjective from the following list:
   My — dog drank all the water in her — bowl.
   big, sad, thirsty, easy, sharp

3. Make a choice from a set of words including adjectives,
   with the child shown where they should go:
   Fill each blank with an adjective from the following list:
   My — dog drank all the water in her — bowl.
   go, hat, big, quickly, thirsty

4. Make a choice from a set of adjectives, with the child not
   shown where they should go:
   Add some adjectives to this sentence from the following
   list:
   My dog drank all the water in her bowl.
   big, sad, thirsty, easy, sharp, cold, wet

5. Allow a completely free choice:
   Add some appropriate adjectives to this sentence:
   My dog drank all the water in her bowl.

For children used to exploring dramatic options, Task 5 offers
a chance to show what they can do (*sweating, disobedient, luke-
warm, shiny* ...), and to use more than one adjective before a
noun. To such children, Task 1 must seem, to say the least,
underwhelming. It tests minimal ability only.

Avoiding the awkward

There is one crucial piece of advice to testers that comes from
descriptive grammar: avoid awkward or contentious examples. A real problem facing anyone who tries to test grammar
is the choice of examples. It's easy enough to identify some

general targets, such as word classes, sentence functions, tense forms, and combining sentences. What's much trickier is to choose sentences that illustrate the point to be tested and which don't present the children with unexpected difficulties. This is where advice from professional grammarians can be of real value.

English grammar isn't like spelling, where most words have a clear-cut correct/incorrect answer: *accommodation* is right; any other version, such as *acomodation*, is wrong. Grammatical rules are only sometimes like that; they frequently present us with exceptions, irregularities, idiosyncrasies. Take the apparently simple rule about 'adding an -*s*' to form a plural noun (p. 29). We might illustrate it with the words *cats*, *dogs*, and *horses*, to show the three kinds of pronunciation that the final -*s* takes. But if we were to choose *houses* instead of *horses*, we would find ourselves faced with an exception. It looks regular, but in fact it isn't, as the *s* of *house* changes its sound to *z* when the plural ending is added. No other noun in the language does this. So it would be unwise to use *houses* as an example of regular plural formation in a test.

Here's an example from a recent test paper for 10-year-olds, which I choose because it displays the kind of problem illustrated by the Lynne Truss debacle I described in Chapter 28, where no attention was paid to context:

> A pair of commas can be used to separate words or groups of words and to clarify the meaning of a sentence. Insert a pair of commas to clarify each sentence below. (a) *My friend who is very fit won the 100-metre race.*

Anyone who has followed the examples in Chapter 28 can see straight away that this sentence is perfectly all right without commas – depending on the intended meaning. It's not a question of clarifying anything. It's the basic distinction, once again, between a restrictive and a non-restrictive relative clause. In *My friend, who is very fit, ...* I have one friend in mind. In *My friend who is very fit ...* I have more than one friend (the other one, who isn't very fit, nonetheless managed to win the egg-and-spoon race). Out of context the question becomes artificial and largely meaningless. But any child in the test who left this sentence without any commas would have been marked wrong.

A different kind of problem arises when a question ignores the existence of language variation. A great deal of online criticism was generated following a test that included the question: 'Which of the sentences below uses commas correctly?' Here were two of the options:

We'll need a board, counters and a pair of dice.
We'll need a board, counters, and a pair of dice.

Only the first of these was accepted as correct. Markers were told in their guidance notes that the so-called 'serial comma' (or 'Oxford comma') was wrong. Evidently the testers had an aversion to serial commas – in which case that's me failed, as I regularly use them (and the whole of Oxford University Press do too, which is where the label comes from). There are, of course, plenty of sentences in English that can illustrate the correct use of a comma, without there being any variation in usage to cause complications. To choose this one illustrates the potential harm that prescriptivism can cause; for in such cases, children will lose marks for innocently following a practice that has a widespread literary presence.

Any test that operates with a narrowly prescriptive approach to grammar can have all kinds of unfortunate consequences, being especially harmful to a child's developing sense of stylistic variation and personal creativity. As the quotation from Robert Graves reminds us (p. 146), it is the 'bending and breaking of rules' that is at the heart of originality in style. Children have to know the rules, but they must also be allowed to show that little extra spark of originality, which should be praised, not penalized. A detailed look at another recent test question shows how easy it is for tests to crush that spark.

Pupils were asked to complete the sentence 'The sun shone — in the sky.' The mark scheme read: 'Accept any appropriate adverb, e.g. brightly, beautifully.' One child presented the answer 'The sun shone dutifully in the sky', and it was marked wrong. The teacher who publicized this example online was understandably upset, and several commented in forums that there was nothing at all wrong with *dutifully*. They saw it as an imaginative way of expressing a situation in a narrative where, for example, after a period of rain, someone begs the sun to appear and it 'dutifully did so'. If this turned up in a story by a well-known author, they suggested, it would be appreciated as a creative use of English and considered to be perfectly appropriate. And indeed, it does turn up, as a few seconds' search on Google will show. Here's an example from an article in the *Independent*:

> 'Oh, I could definitely live here,' said one enthralled
> visitor as the sun shone dutifully through a wall of picture
> windows.

Of course, we don't know why the child who gave the answer used that particular adverb. I'm assuming, like the teacher, who knew the child, that he or she was being consciously creative; but, of course, it's also possible that a child might write *dutifully* without any thought as to its appropriateness. So one of the ways in which grammar tests of this kind can be made more meaningful and involving would be to provide a space for pupils to give explanations about why they make the choices they make – a pragmatic perspective. To reject it in a test out of hand is to convey to children and their teachers that the only kind of English that testers want to see is of a predictable, clichéd, and uninspiring kind.

'The sun shone — in the sky' is also another example of an 'awkward case' that isn't immediately apparent. The difficulty surfaced quickly when another child presented the answer 'The sun shone bright in the sky', and this was marked wrong, on the grounds that *bright* is 'not an adverb'. The testers were clearly interpreting 'appropriate' to mean 'appropriate to the rules prescriptive grammarians think operate in English', where *brightly* would, of course, be privileged. It has been the norm in formal written standard English for the last couple of centuries. But if you take 'appropriate' to mean 'in a way that makes sense', then *bright* is a perfectly normal alternative, used adverbially by hundreds of millions all over the English-speaking world, in writing as well as in speech.

It has been a part of English since Anglo-Saxon times. You'll find an adverbial use of *bright* in *Beowulf*, in Chaucer, in Shakespeare (repeatedly – 'The moon shines bright', 'teach the torches to burn bright'), and right down to the present day. Prescriptive grammarians took against it in the eighteenth century, but they were unable to stop the usage. An idiomatic adverbial use of *bright* is used even by prescriptively minded people, when they say such things as 'I got up bright and early.' Henry Watson Fowler, beloved of prescriptivists, saw the nonsense. In the entry in his *Dictionary of Modern English Usage* (1926) on what he calls 'unidiomatic -ly' we find: 'much more to be deprecated ... is the growing notion that every monosyllabic adjective, if an adverb is to be made of it, must have a *-ly* clapped on it to proclaim the fact', and he condemns the 'ignorance' that leads people to think in this way.

There is, of course, nothing wrong with the aim of teaching the basic piece of grammatical knowledge that lies behind this question. Many adjectives can be turned into adverbs by adding *-ly*, and knowledge of this rule can extend children's expressive repertoire, and help them appreciate the stylistic difference between standard and nonstandard English. But there are several adjectives it would be wise to avoid in a test, as they add complications. *High* can add *-ly* to become *highly*, but not with the same meaning. *Good* can add *-ly* yet stays an adjective (*a goodly sum*).

The sentence selected for the test was one of those awkward cases, because our intuitions about what is appropriate are also being pulled in the direction of other sentences where adjectives would be perfectly normal, as these examples illustrate:

The boy feels happy. = The happy boy.
The sun shines bright(ly). = The bright sun.

Children who think of the brightness as applying to the sun rather than to the act of shining would be thinking adjectivally, and this would motivate them to choose *bright*. The test-setters, of course, were thinking of the brightness only in relation to the action of the verb, so for them the only option was *brightly*. The bad decision, on their part, was to go for a sentence that was being pulled in two directions at once. It should never have been chosen. But that requires quite a bit of grammatical awareness, which plainly was missing. And, as always with badly chosen questions, it's the children who pay the price (along with their confused parents). It is that kind of undesirable outcome that a linguistically informed grammatical pedagogy seeks to avoid.

References and further reading

My approach to grammar is expounded in its fullest form in the two reference grammars written by Randolph Quirk, Sidney Greenbaum, Geoffrey Leech, and Jan Svartvik, *A Grammar of Contemporary English* (Longman, 1972) and *A Comprehensive Grammar of the English Language* (Longman, 1985).

Shorter versions include Quirk and Greenbaum, *A University Grammar of English* (Longman, 1973), Greenbaum and Quirk, *A Student's Grammar of the English Language* (Longman, 1990), and Leech and Svartvik, *A Communicative Grammar of English* (Longman, 2nd edn, 1994).

My *Rediscover Grammar* (Longman, 1988, 3rd edn, 2004) is an elementary introduction to this approach, later accompanied by a schools textbook *Discover Grammar* (Longman, 1996, with classroom consultant Geoff Barton). *Making Sense of Grammar* (Longman, 2004) adds the semantic and pragmatic perspectives to this approach, following the chapter-organization of *Rediscover Grammar*. The role of punctuation in relation to grammar is explored in my *Making a Point: the Pernickety Story of English Punctuation* (Profile, 2015).

Related books include Douglas Biber, Stig Johansson, Geoffrey Leech, Susan Conrad, and Edward Finegan, *Longman Grammar of Spoken and Written English* (Longman, 1999), and

Douglas Biber, Susan Conrad, and Geoffrey Leech, *Longman Student Grammar of Spoken and Written English* (Longman, 2002).

Other important grammars include Rodney Huddleston and Geoffrey K. Pullum, and others, *The Cambridge Grammar of the English Language* (Cambridge University Press, 2002), Ronald Carter and Michael McCarthy, *Cambridge Grammar of English* (Cambridge University Press, 2006), and Bas Aarts, *Oxford Modern English Grammar* (Oxford University Press, 2011). Related to the Survey of English Usage is *The Internet Grammar of English* http://www.ucl.ac.uk/internet-grammar and *Englicious* www.englicious.org.

The research studies that informed Chapter 20 can be followed up in Sandra Mollin, 'Revisiting binomial order in English: ordering constraints and reversibility', *English Language and Linguistics* 16(1), 2012, 81–103.

History of Grammar

R. H. Robins, *A Short History of Linguistics* (Longman, 1967).
Francis P. Dinneen, *An Introduction to General Linguistics* (Holt, Rinehart and Winston, 1967).

History of English

David Crystal, *The Stories of English* (Penguin, 2004).
David Crystal, *English as a Global Language* (Cambridge University Press, 2nd edn, 2003).
Richard M. Hogg and David Denison (eds), *A History of the English Language* (Cambridge University Press, 2006).
Lynda Mugglestone (ed.), *The Oxford History of English* (Oxford University Press, 2006).

Background to English Usage and Variation

David Crystal, *The Fight for English* (Oxford University Press, 2006).

David Crystal, *The Cambridge Encyclopedia of the English Language* (Cambridge University Press, 2nd edn, 2003).

David Crystal and Derek Davy, *Investigating English Style* (Longman, 1969).

Henry Hitchings, *The Language Wars: A History of Proper English* (Murray, 2011).

Oliver Kamm, *Accidence Will Happen: The Non-pedantic Guide to English Usage* (Weidenfeld and Nicolson, 2015).

Pam Peters, *The Cambridge Guide to English Usage* (Cambridge University Press, 2004).

Steven Pinker, *The Sense of Style* (Allen Lane, 2014).

English Today (Cambridge University Press, quarterly).

Grammar in education

David Crystal, 'The recent political history of English grammar in the UK', in the Books and Articles section of www.davidcrystal.com

Peter Doughty, John Pearce, and Geoffrey Thornton, *Language in Use* (Edward Arnold, 1971).

Richard Hudson, *Teaching Grammar* (Blackwell, 1992).

Richard Hudson and John Walmsley, 'The English Patient: English grammar and teaching in the twentieth century', *Journal of Linguistics* 41(3), 2005, 593–622. http://dickhudson.com/papers/#patient

Carl James and Peter Garrett (eds), *Language Awareness in the Classroom* (Longman, 1991).

Debra Myhill and Annabel Watson, 'The role of grammar in the writing curriculum: a review of the literature', *Child Language Teaching and Therapy*, 30(1), 2014, 41–62.

Laurence Walker, *200 Years of Grammar: A History of Grammar Teaching in Canada, New Zealand, and Australia, 1800–2000* (iUniverse, 2011).

The Bullock Report: *A Language for Life* (HMSO, 1975). http://www.educationengland.org.uk/documents/bullock/bullock1975.html

The Cox Report: *English for Ages 5 to 16* (HMSO, 1989). http://www.educationengland.org.uk/documents/cox1989/cox89.html

The Kingman Report: *Report of the Committee of Inquiry into the Teaching of the English Language* (HMSO, 1988). http://www.educationengland.org.uk/documents/kingman/kingman1988.html

The Newbolt Report: *The Teaching of English in England* (HMSO, 1921). http://www.educationengland.org.uk/documents/newbolt/newbolt1921.html

Language acquisition and teaching materials

David Crystal, *Language A to Z*, two student books and teachers book (Longman, 1991), new edition with combined student books (available at www.davidcrystal.com).

David Crystal, *Listen to Your Child* (Penguin, 1986).

David Crystal and Jeff Bevington, *Skylarks: A Language Development Library for 6- to 9-year-olds* (Nelson, 1975).

David Crystal, Paul Fletcher, and Michael Garman, *The Grammatical Analysis of Language Disability* (Edward Arnold, 1976); available from the University of Canterbury, Christchurch at http://ir.canterbury.ac.nz/

handle/10092/5483; the associated workbook, *Working with LARSP*, is also available at this site.

David Crystal and John Foster, *Databank* series (Arnold, 1979–85), *Datasearch* series (Arnold, 1991).

Bridie Raban, *The Spoken Vocabulary of Five-year-old Children* (School of Education, University of Reading, 1988).

Lindsey Thomas, *The Buckinghamshire Grammar Project* (2014). http://bucksgrammar.weebly.com

Illustration credits

39. Taken from J. R. Turner, *The Works of William Bullokar* (University of Leeds, 1980)
49, 88, 99, 202. Author's collection
80. Photograph by Hilary Crystal
107. © Plain English Campaign
240. © Sidney Harris

Index